Hammond Synchronous Clocks

Maintenance and Repair

by Craig Shields

Hammond Synchronous Clocks Maintenance and Repair

A Clock Press Book
copyright © 2011 by Craig Shields
published by Clock Press

ISBN: 978-0-9846718-0-9

All Rights Reserved. No part of this book may be reproduced or transmitted in any form or by any means, electronic or mechanical, including photocopying, recording or by any information storage and retrieval system, without written permission from the publisher.

Published in the United States by Clock Press, Kansas City, Kansas.
www.clockpress.com

Disclaimer
This book is designed to provide information about disassembly, cleaning, oiling, replacing cords and re-assembly of a variety of Hammond Electric Clocks. It is sold with the understanding that the author is not engaged in rendering professional clock repair services and is an amateur repairman-collector providing information intended for other hobbyists. If expert repair assistance is required, the services of a competent clock care professional should be sought.

It is not the purpose of this manual to reprint all the information that is otherwise available to clock collectors and clock repair people but to complement, amplify and supplement other texts. This book does not attempt to cover all possible variations of Hammond Clock movements, motors, cases or assemblies. For more information, see the many references in the bibliography.

Every effort has been made to make this book as complete and as accurate as possible. However, there may be mistakes both typographical and in content. Therefore, this text should be used only as a general guide and not as the ultimate source of clock repair and collecting.

The purpose of this manual is to educate and entertain. The author and publisher shall have neither liability nor responsibility to any person or entity with respect to any loss or damage caused or alleged to be caused directly or indirectly by the information contained in this book.

Finally, the reader is encouraged to practice the techniques shown in this book on damaged or otherwise low value, salvage grade clocks to gain experience before attempting repairs on their most prized clocks.

Table of Contents

Chapter 1 - Introduction - 1

    1   Welcome to Hammond Synchronous Clocks
    2   Identify the Open Rotor Movement
    3   Identify the Sealed Rotor
    4   How Synchronous Clocks Show the Time
    5   When You Need the Help of a Clockmaker
    6   A Brief History of the Hammond Clock Company
    7   Tools

Chapter 2 - Open Rotor Clock Disassembly - Postal Telegraph SX15 - 5

    1   The Clock
    2   Remove the Backer Board
    3   Remove the Bezel
    4   Bezel Tabs - Correct Usage
    5   Bezel Tabs - Incorrect Usage
    6   Bezel Removal
    7   Removing the Second Hand
    8   Remove the Minute Hand
    9   Remove the Hour Hand
    10   Remove the Set Time Knob
    11   Remove the Start Knob
    12   Free the Motor from the Case
    13   Remove the Motor Dust Cover
    14   Remove the Mounting Flange
    15   Separate the Plates
    16   Examine the Arrangement of Gears
    17   Examine the Back Plate and Bushings
    18   Front Plate and Hour Wheel
    19   The Rotor
    20   The Start Wheel
    21   The Set Time Gears
    22   The Center Wheels
    23   The Minutes and Seconds Gears
    24   Disassembly Complete

Chapter 3 - Replacing the Power Cord - 15

    1   Checking the Coil
    2   The Field and Coil
    3   Mark the Coil
    4   Remove the Field and Core
    5   Open the Paper Wrapping
    6   Expose the Leads
    7   Trim the Magnet Wire
    8   Ready for New Cord
    9   A not so Clean Example
    10   Messy Coil after Cleanup
    11   Prepare the New Cord
    12   Support the Coil
    13   Make Connections and Solder
    14   Wrap with Tape to Complete
    15   Summary

Chapter 4 - Cleaning the Open Rotor Movement - 21

1. Cleaning the Case
2. Cleaning the Dial
3. General Cleaning of the Gears
4. Cleaning the Rotor
5. Cleaning the Fiber Gear
6. Cleaning the Minute/Sec Gears
7. Cleaning the Plates
8. Summary

Chapter 5 - Oiling the Open Rotor Movement - 25

1. Oiling the Rotor
2. Oiling the Set Gears - 1
3. Oiling the Set Gears - 2
4. Oiling the Set Gears - 3
5. Oiling the Minute Wheel and Pinion
6. Oiling the Minute Wheel Base
7. Oiling the Seconds Shaft
8. Oiling the Hour Wheel Base
9. Oiling the Hour Wheel Cannon
10. Oiling the Bushings - 1
11. Oiling the Bushings - 2
12. Oiling the Bushings - 3
13. Oiling the Bushings - 4
14. Oiling the Bushings - 5
15. Oiling the Bushings - 6
16. Oiling the Bushings - 7
17. Oiling the Bushings - 8

Chapter 6 - Open Rotor Clock Assembly - Postal Telegraph SX15 - 33

1. Install the Field/Coil
2. Install the Rotor
3. Install the Start Wheel
4. Install the Set Gears
5. Install the Min/Sec Gears
6. Side View of Installed Gears
7. Install the Front Plate
8. Secure the Plates
9. Install the Motor and Knobs
10. Install the Dial
11. Install the Hands
12. Install the Glass
13. Install the Bezel Ring
14. Install the Backer Board
15. Assembly Complete

Chapter 7 - Disassembly and Reassembly — "Gregory" Desk Clock with Calendar - 39

1. The Gregory
2. Remove the Outer Case
3. Remove the Case Back
4. Remove the Sealed Rotor Unit
5. Remove the Hands
6. Remove the Dial
7. Separate the Plates
8. Remove the Wheels for Cleaning
9. Oiling the Minutes Gear
10. Assembling the Gear Train
11. Calendar Synchronization and Final Assembly
12. Polishing the Bakelite Case

Chapter 8 - Sealed Rotor Treatment - 45
- 1 Sealed Rotor Unit
- 2 Opening the Seal
- 3 Pry up the Stopper
- 4 Treatment for Dried Oil
- 5 Clean up and Reseal

Opening the Rotor
- 1 Soak and Clean
- 2 Oiling
- 3 Reassembly

Bibliography - 51

Hammond Clock Company Ephemera - 53
- 54 Punch Card Premium - Undated
- 55 Hammond Clock Company Stock Certificate
- 56 Premium Punch Card 1933
- 57 Hammond Sealed Rotor Conversion Kit Instructions
- 61 Hammond Sealed Rotor Conversion Kit Warranty Post Card
- 62 Two Clocks in One Brochure
- 66 Exact Time Brochure
- 70 Modern Time Brochure

Hammond Clock Company Patent Drawings - 75

76	July 6, 1920	Utility Patent	Clock
77	July 2, 1929	Utility Patent	Alternating Current Clock
78	March 24, 1931	Utility Patent	Alternating Current Clock
79	December 25, 1934	Utility Patent	Calendar Clock
80	May 21, 1935	Utility Patent	Electric Timepiece
81	May 28, 1935	Utility Patent	Electric Clock Motor
82	September 3, 1935	Utility Patent	Electric Clock
83	January 14, 1936	Utility Patent	Electric Alarm Clock
84	May 26, 1936	Utility Patent	Calendar Clock
85	January 12, 1937	Utility Patent	Electric Clock
86	December 31, 1940	Utility Patent	Illuminated Dial Clock
87	April 28, 1942	Utility Patent	Clock
88	August 26, 1930	Utility Patent	Synchronous Motor
89	May 26, 1931	Design Patent	Clock Case
90	September 1, 1931	Design Patent	Clock Dial
91	September 1, 1931	Design Patent	Clock Case
92	September 8, 1931	Design Patent	Clock Case
93	September 8, 1931	Design Patent	Clock Case
94	December 8, 1931	Design Patent	Combined Dial and Hands
95	December 8, 1931	Design Patent	Combined Dial and Hands
96	March 15, 1932	Design Patent	Clock Case
97	November 29, 1932	Utility Patent	Card Table

Chapter 1 - Introduction

1   Welcome
2   How to Identify the Open Rotor Movement
3   How to Identify the Sealed Rotor Movement
4   How Synchronous Clocks Show the Time
5   When You Need the Help of a Clockmaker
6   A Brief History of the Hammond Clock Company
7   Tools

Open Rotor - Back Plate

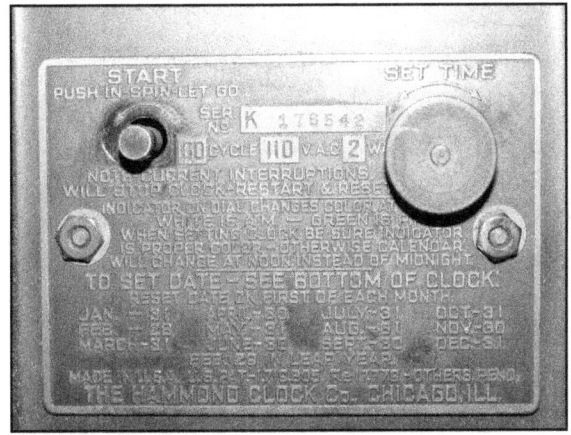

Sealed Rotor - Back Plate

1 Welcome to Hammond Synchronous Clocks

This book is a collection of my notes and experience collecting Hammond Clocks. This book is written for the collector to fill the gaps in knowledge of how to maintain Hammond clocks. The focus of this book is on the most common repairs: cleaning, oiling and replacing cords. The book was written with the Hammond clock collector in mind. Over 100 photographs show those jobs and procedures that an amateur can easily and safely accomplish while maintaining and or increasing the value of his or her clock collection. **Please read and understand all instruction steps in a chapter before starting your repair project.** This book covers Hammond synchronous motors in the two most common flavors, open rotor and sealed rotor. Most often these clocks simply need cleaning and fresh oil to continue running. The reader will be able to apply the procedures in this book to many styles of Hammond Clock because while the cases are different, most Hammond clocks employ one of two types of motors, open rotor and sealed rotor synchronous. Due to their complexity, Hammond Bichronous clock motors are out of the scope of this amateur repair book as discussed below.

2 How to Identify the Open Rotor Movement

The open rotor style of movement is the most common motor used in Hammond clocks. The photo on the right shows the back plate of an open rotor style movement of the kind we work on in this book. It is easy to disassemble, clean and oil. Notice the circular form. Notice the shielded start knob. Notice the bulging area for the coil. These are identifying characteristics of the Hammond Open Rotor style movement. Any clock you see with this style of plate in back uses a Hammond movement and is easily maintained by the amateur collector.

3 How to Identify the Sealed Rotor Movement

This photo shows the back of the "Gregory" Hammond clock and is typical of the sealed rotor style. Notice the large set time knob with threaded center hole. Notice that the start knob is small enough to go through the hole in the back plate. Notice the 2 nuts holding the data plate. The size of the data plate varies, this being a larger plate. These are the identifying characteristics of Hammond sealed rotor movement clocks.

4 How Synchronous Clocks Show the Time

A wind up clock uses spring power regulated by a pendulum (or balance wheel) and escapement to keep it's own time, fast or slow. It has an internal way of determining the passage of time (pendulum swing) and does not depend upon any external help or signal to keep time.

A synchronous clock is a simple electric motor. It shows the time by using a series of gears, rotated by alternating currents sent from the power company at 60hz. The 60hz nationwide standard frequency is regulated by the generating equipment at the power utility company. When a synchronous clock is running it will keep in perfect synchronization with the frequency sent to your home from the utility, thus synchronous clocks are accurate to within several seconds, depending on the **Time Error Corrections** made by the power utility each day. The synchronous clock does not provide for regulation of time like a wind up clock; **regulation is provided by the power utility**.

Note: As of 2011, the NERC (North American Electric Reliability Corporation) is investigating the possibility of eliminating Time Error Corrections which would reduce the long-term accuracy of clocks (and other devices) that use the 60 Hz frequency as a time base. If implemented, this change could mean that Hammond clock owners would need to monitor the accuracy of their clocks and possibly make periodic adjustments to keep in time. Google the phrase "nerc time error corrections" for more information.

5 When You Need the Help of a Clockmaker

Bichronous clocks are more complex than synchronous. They do have an internal method of time regulation and they contain springs under tension. For these reasons, repair of the Bichronous movement is best left to Clockmaking professionals and is out of the scope of this book.

Another issue that often plagues synchronous clocks is worn rotor bushings. Hammond clock motors are strong and will run a long time while dirty which will wear out the bushings. You will notice that the clock frequently stops or won't run at all. Upon examining the rotor bushings you will note that the bushing holes are out of round or "egg shaped". To correct this condition is a repair that requires special equipment and thus should be sent to your professional Clockmaker.

6 A Brief History of The Hammond Clock Company

Laurens Hammond, founder of the company, was working on a "tickless" clock design in the late teens and early 1920's, securing patents for clock devices before 1925. The Hammond Clock Company was formed and began making clocks in the late 1920's. Around about 1937 the company name changed to Hammond Instrument company, reflecting the company focus on musical instruments. (This company name change date can be useful in dating clocks in your collection). Sometime in the early 1940's Hammond stopped making clocks altogether and focused exclusively on musical instruments, going on to make the still popular Hammond B-3 Organ and later aquiring rights to the Leslie rotating speaker system.

7 Tools

These are the tools and supplies you will need to complete all of the projects outlined in this book. Optional cleaning solutions, pegwood, pithwood and the other clock repair specific items may be obtained at any well stocked clock repair supply dealer.

- Long Nose Pliers
- Flat Blade Screwdriver
- 7/32" Nut Driver
- 5/16" Nut Driver
- 1/4" Nut Driver
- Pen
- Butter Knife
- Paper Towels
- Clock Hand Removal Tool (optional)
- OHM Meter (optional)
- Marker
- Razor Knife
- Small Wire Snips
- Wire Stripper
- Vise
- Soldering Iron
- Solder
- Electrical Tape
- 18/2 Lamp Cord
- Toothpicks
- Pegwood (optional)
- Pithwood Buttons (optional)
- Small Soft Bristle Brush
- Parts Scrubbing Brush
- Parts or Clock Cleaning Solution
- Propane Torch
- Denatured Alcohol
- Blow Dryer or other Heated Forced Air
- Light oil or Clock oil
- Jars or Containers for Cleaning Solution
- Paper Wire Ties
- Paper Towels
- Clock Oiling Tool (optional)

Chapter 2
Open Rotor Clock Disassembly
Postal Telegraph SX15

Postal Telegraph SX15

Open Rotor Movement

1. The Clock
2. Remove the Backer Board
3. Remove the Bezel
4. Bezel Tabs - Correct Usage
5. Bezel Tabs - Incorrect Usage
6. Bezel Removal
7. Removing the Second Hand
8. Remove the Minute Hand
9. Remove the Hour Hand
10. Remove the Set Time Knob
11. Remove the Start Knob
12. Free the Motor from the Case
13. Remove the Motor Dust Cover
14. Remove the Mounting Flange
15. Separate the Plates
16. Examine the Arrangement of Gears
17. Examine the Back Plate and Bushings
18. Front Plate and Hour Wheel
19. The Rotor
20. The Start Wheel
21. The Set Time Gears
22. The Center Wheels
23. The Minutes and Seconds Gears
24. Disassembly Complete

1. The Postal Telegraph Clock by Hammond

The clock we are working on is the Postal Telegraph Synchronous Electric Time, model SX15, manufactured for Postal Telegraph by Hammond Instrument Company sometime after 1937. Earlier clocks of the same design will indicate the company name as Hammond Clock Company. The design of the older and later models is identical. This is a large clock, measuring 19$^{3/4}$" across with a 15" dial. This clock uses the Hammond Open Rotor Synchronous Electric motor that is common to millions of Hammond clocks. Let's begin dis-assembly by removing the backer board.

2. Remove the Backer Board

To begin disassembly, turn the clock over onto a sturdy work surface. Take care not to mar the chrome bezel ring. Remove the three screws holding the back cover board. This backer board is missing on many clocks. Next, unlock the bezel ring tabs.

3. Remove the Bezel

With the backer board removed locate and straighten the six metal bezel ring tabs extending through the case slots located at 12, 2, 4, 6, 8 and 10. These tabs are fragile and require careful handling in order to preserve them. Now examine one of the bezel ring tabs up close.

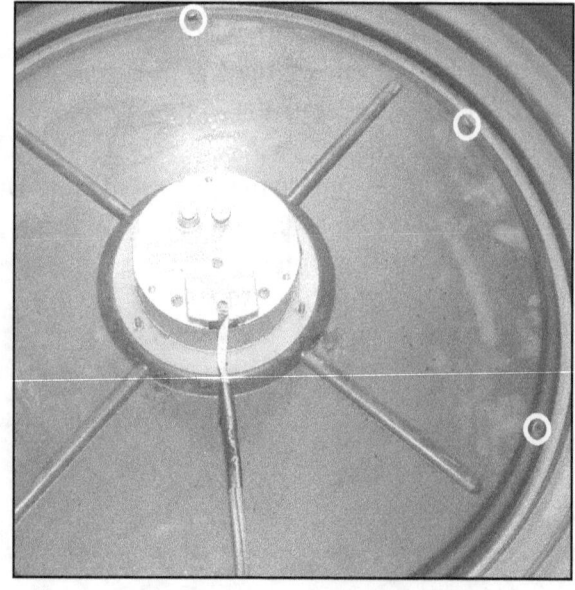

4. Bezel Tabs - Correct Usage

Close-up of a chrome bezel ring tab and it's slot. The tab is twisted slightly in order to hold it in place by friction. This is the correct way to secure these metal tabs. Twisting the tab minimizes the amount of flexing on the metal and lengthens the life of the bezel ring. Now let's see how NOT to bend a bezel ring tab.

5. Bezel Tabs - Incorrect Usage

Here the tab is bent over at nearly a 90 degree angle. This will eventually ruin the bezel ring by breaking off the metal tabs. These tabs are fragile. They will crack and eventually break off due to flexing. Do not bend the tabs over in this manner. Now that the tabs are straightened, remove the bezel ring from the case.

6. Bezel Removal

After straightening the tabs, turn the clock face up and lift the bezel ring. It may be necessary to push on the tabs from under the clock to raise the bezel. Once the bezel is free, hang it up out of the way. Now remove the glass to a safe place. **The glass is 15$^{3/4}$" diameter**. If you need replacement glass, be sure to specify double strength thickness when ordering from your glazier. Now you are ready to remove the clock hands.

7. Removing the Second Hand

While you are removing the hands the most important thing is to not scratch or mar the dial in any way. Avoid touching the dial with your bare fingers. First, unthread the second hand from it's post by holding the start knob at the back of the clock while gently turning the second hand counter clockwise. The second hand is actually two pieces, the flat metal shape and a central threaded nut.

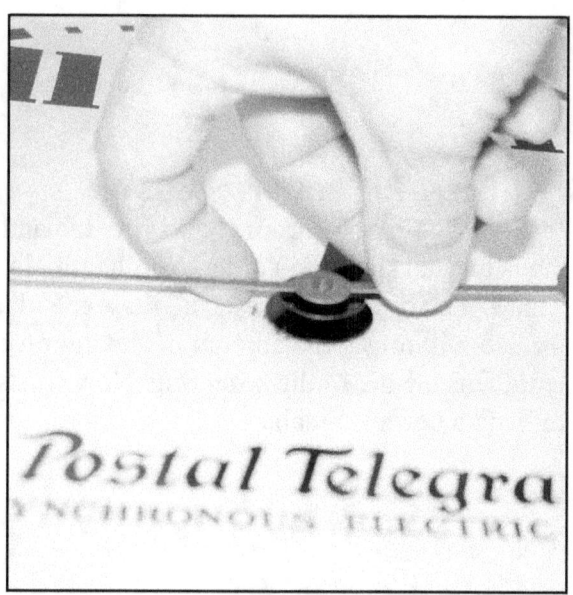

8. Remove the Minute Hand

To remove the minute hand, hold the hand steady and use a 7/32" nut driver to loosen the nut holding the hand to the shaft. When reinstalling the nut, always start it by hand. It is easy to get this small nut crooked on the fine threads. The minute hand has a rectangular hole. This will allow you to perfectly align the hands during reassembly. Next, remove the hour hand.

9. Remove the Hour Hand

To remove the hour hand, lift it using a butter knife to lift, a towel to protect the face and a pen or suitable size dowel for leverage. The hour hand is friction fit and may suddenly pop off it's post if it is very tight, otherwise it will gradually lift off of the hour "cannon". The hour hand is actually two pieces, the flat metal shape and a round bushing that fits over the hour cannon. Now the dial is free to be removed. Hang the dial by the center hole to keep it safe. Notice the small locator holes in the dial at 12 and 6 and the small locator bumps on the case to allow precise positioning during re-assembly.

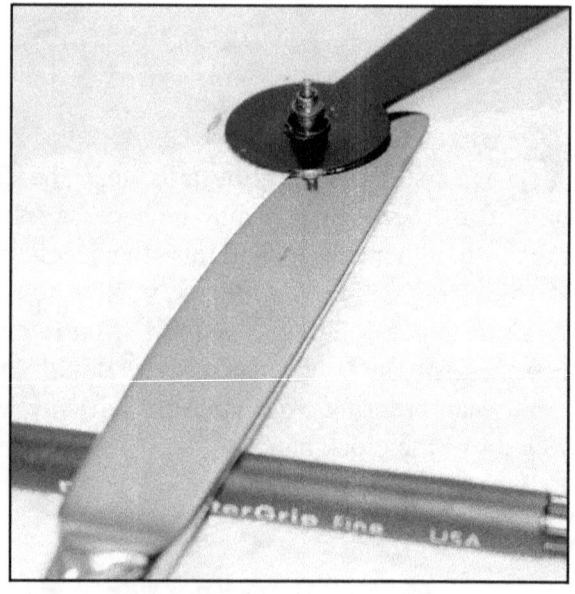

10. Remove the Set Time Knob

Use the butter knife, pen and towel as shown to remove the knobs from the back of the movement. Use an upward prying motion to lift the knob off the shaft. You may also use a clock hand removal tool for both removing the hands and these knobs. S. LaRose can supply this and other tools you may find useful in maintaining your collection. Next, remove the start knob.

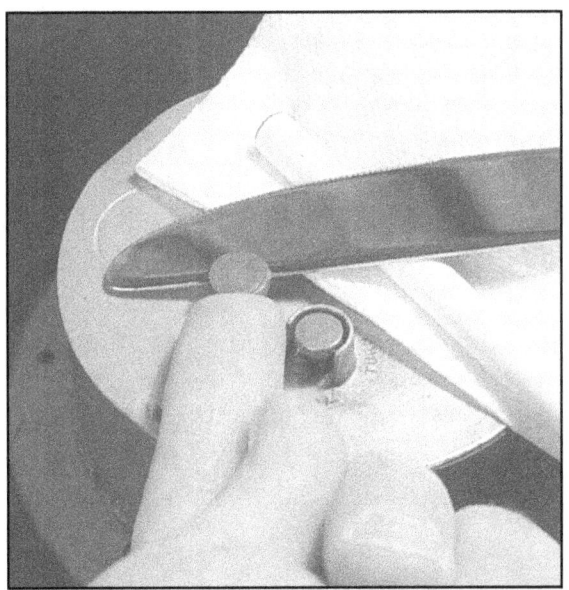

11. Remove the Start Knob

This one is a little more difficult due to the motion shield. Removing the knobs is much easier while the movement is still attached to the case. The purchase of a clock hand removal tool, such as shown in the next panel, will greatly aid you in removing hands and knobs, especially if you have many clocks to maintain. Now we are ready to free the motor from the clock case.

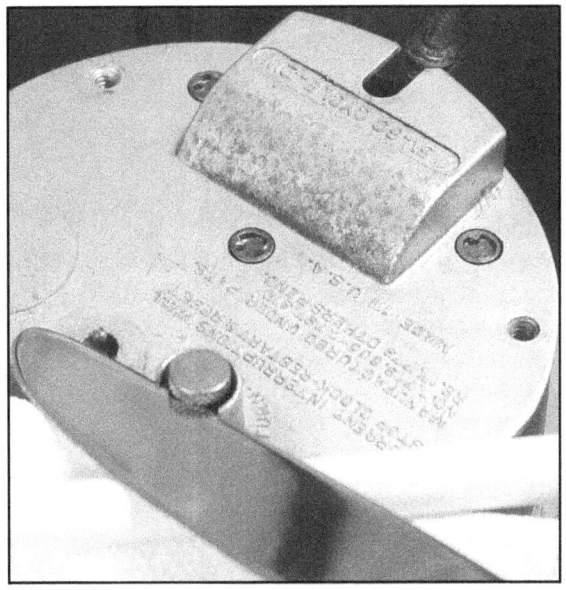

A clock hand removal tool is very handy in removing knobs and hands. Any clock tools supplier will have a selection. As demonstrated above, this tool is optional.

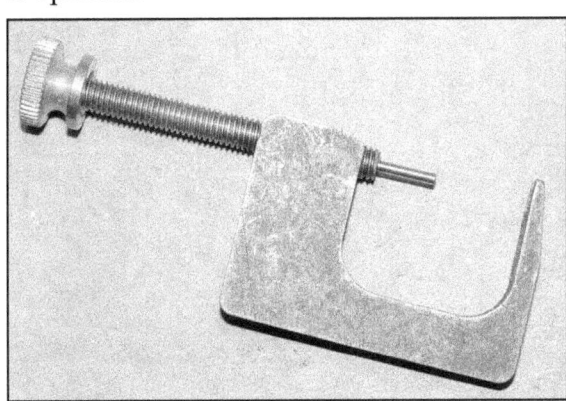

12 Free the Motor from the Case

To free the motor from the case, lift the case and hold the movement underneath while loosening the 3 screws that attach the movement mounting flange to the case. Hold the nut on the bottom side while turning with the screwdriver. You may be able to turn the nut with your fingers once it is loose. Now the motor is free from the clock case, with the mounting flange still attached. Now we will remove the dust cover from the motor.

13 Remove the Motor Dust Cover

To remove the motor dust cover, unhook the tab from the metal dust cover sleeve, unwrap the metal sleeve and set it aside. Next, remove the mounting flange and separate the front and back plates of the clock motor.

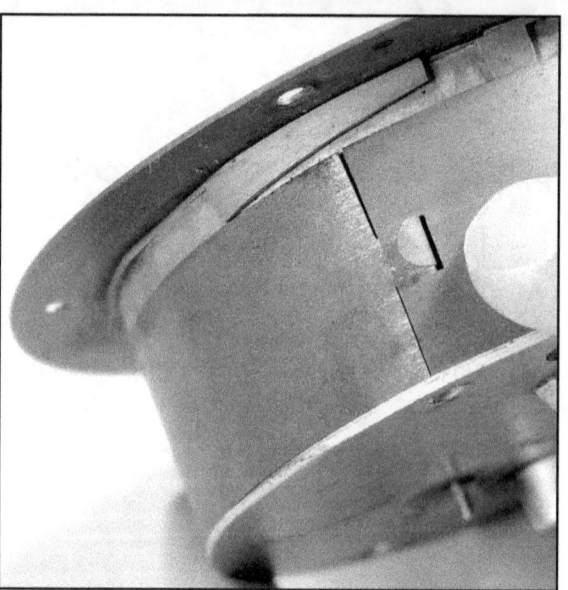

14 Remove the Mounting Flange

To remove the mounting flange and separate the plates, remove the 3 screws holding the metal flange. These screws also hold the plates together. The flange ring serves to attach the clock motor to the case. The plates are fit together fairly snug at the bosses, so the motor won't come apart just yet. Set the flange aside and prepare for separation.

15 Separate the Plates

To separate the front and back motor plates and expose the gears, hold the bottom plate while gently lifting upward to separate the two plates. Now, with the front plate removed, lay the back plate down on the table with the gears in place and examine the motor in detail.

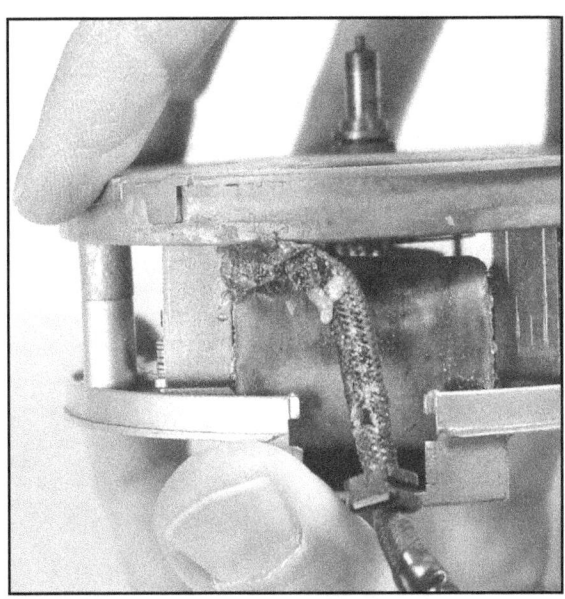

16 Examine the Arrangement of Gears

Here is the motor with the front plate removed. This shows how you will position the gears for reassembly. The gears are numbered. Number one is the rotor which is driven by the electric current flowing through the field or stator. The rotor wheel has 32 poles and spins at 225 RPM. Number two is the phenol/fiber gear. This is the gear connected to the start knob in back. This fiber gear imparts the starting motion to the rotor wheel. Number 3 is the setting gears. It is connected to the set knob in back. Number 4 is the minutes and seconds wheels. It is actually two gears, one inside the other, which will be discussed later. Now remove the gears and examine the back motor plate.

17 Examine the Back Plate and Bushings

The gears are now removed showing the back plate of the motor. The gears are placed around the movement in relative position to their bearing holes. Notice the bearing points for each of the 4 arbors. (The arbor is the metal rod that supports the gears and pinions.) Arbors 2 and 3 protrude through the back plate and have knobs attached during normal operation. Number 2 is the "Start" knob, number 3 is the "Set Time" knob. Arbor 4 is the minutes and seconds wheel and it extends through the front plate by passing through the center of the hour wheel. See the next image for the hour wheel and front plate.

18 Front Plate and Hour Wheel

This is the inside of the front plate. The kidney shaped hole is always over the coil on this style of movement. The large wheel in the center is the hour wheel. It is attached to the hour "cannon" which extends through to the other side of this plate and onto which the hour hand is fitted. The hour wheel itself is captive to the front plate and is not removed in the procedures outlined in this book. The numbers correspond to the respective numbered arbors and bushings identified above. Now let's examine each of the 4 wheels in detail.

19. The Rotor

This is the rotor wheel. The parts we need to know about are the torsion spring and the brass weight. The spring connects the weight to the wheel and provides a forward momentum to smooth out the motion during starting and running. The spring has two hooks, one at it's lower edge where it contacts the weight between the pinion leaves, the other at the top where it connects between the small pinion. Hold the steel rotor while gently turning the brass weight then let go to demonstrate the spring action.

20. The Start Wheel

This is the 60 tooth start wheel, made of fiber and phenol resin. It is strong and lightweight but can be broken. This wheel takes your spin motion and turns the rotor which then starts spinning at 225 RPM due to the number of poles on the rotor and the current generated by the coil. Damage to this wheel is unfortunate because this material will be difficult, if not impossible, to repair. Luckily, many Hammond clocks contain similar wheels of the exact same size which may be used should you encounter damage to this part of your clock motor. A cylindrical spacer sets the proper spacing for the start knob attachment.

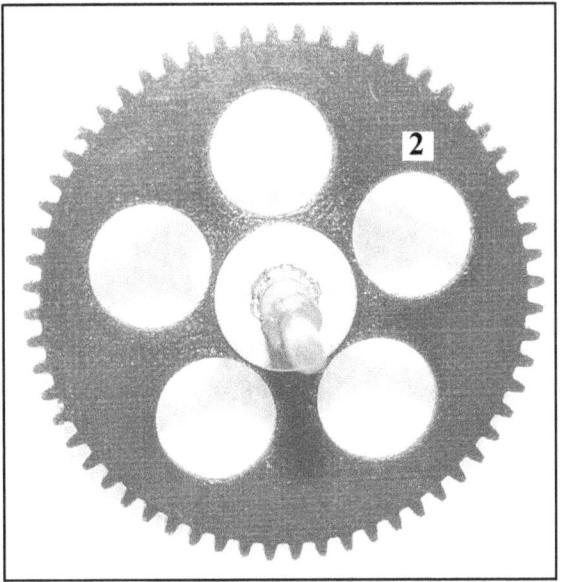

21. The Set Time Gears

This wheel set imparts the motion of setting the time to the other gears in the motor. The top gear is directly connected to the arbor and the other two gears ride on the arbor. To check it's operation hold the top gear while spinning the bottom two, then hold the bottom two while spinning the top. Note the cylindrical spacer under the bottom gear. This provides the spacing between the clock plate and the bottom of the gear, allowing for the correct length of the arbor to extend out the back of the motor for the set knob. Be sure these turn freely when assembling the motor after oiling.

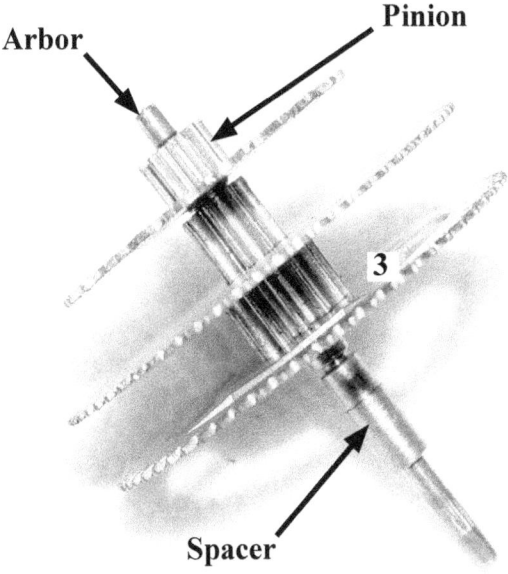

22 The Center Wheels

This is the center gear set. It carries the minute and seconds wheels. It is in two pieces, the seconds wheel arbor riding inside the minute wheel shaft. The seconds arbor is threaded at the end to accept the second hand. The minute shaft is squared at the end to accept the minute hand and retaining nut. Not all Hammond clocks have this arrangement. Some of the smaller wall and desk clock models will have friction fit hands. We will now separate this assembly.

23 The Minutes and Seconds Gears

This shows the minute and seconds gears separated. Notice the triangular shaped washer on the bottom of the minute wheel. This is actually a flat spring washer intended to maintain some friction between the minute wheel pinion and it's larger toothed wheel. You can turn this spring slightly to get under it for cleaning, but be very careful not to bend or distort it at all. You want to be able to turn the large pinion separate of the gear without freewheeling or sticking. Normally this is no problem and no special adjustments are made here. When oiling be sure the pinion turns smoothly.

24 Disassembly Complete

Disassembly is now complete. Your Hammond clock is now ready for the following services: electric cord replacement, cleaning, oiling and reassembly. Please move on to the next section of this manual to being replacing the electrical cord. This is also a good time to review what you have done so far and to organize the parts we have accumulated during the disassembly process. Assembling the clock is easier if all the parts are neatly organized and easily at hand when you need them. If you plan to have your case parts plated or painted now is the time to package them for shipping or transport to your painter or plating service. Check Hemmings Motor News magazine for sources on plating metal parts if you are unable to locate these services locally. If it will be some time before you reassemble your clock, package and label the parts for storage to prevent loss or mix-ups.

Chapter 3
Replacing the Power Cord

1   Checking the Coil
2   The Field and Coil
3   Mark the Coil
4   Remove the Field and Core
5   Open the Paper Wrapping
6   Expose the Leads
7   Trim the Magnet Wire
8   Ready for New Cord
9   A not so Clean Example
10   Messy Coil after Cleanup
11   Prepare the New Cord
12   Support the Coil
13   Make Connections and Solder
14   Wrap with Tape to Complete
15   Summary

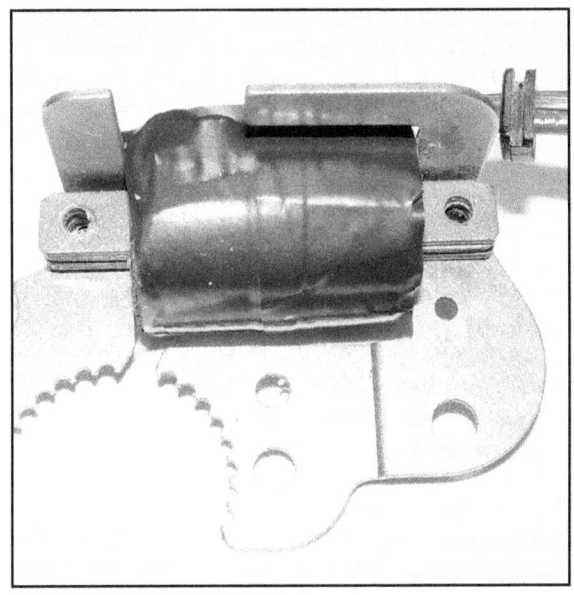

1. Checking the Coil

If your clock has not worked at all and showed no signs of power (by at least trying to run) when you tried to start it, you should check the coil now. Use a simple Volt-Ohm meter, set the range to ohms x10, and put one test probe on either side of the cut ends of the power cord, or even on the power plug prongs while the cord is still attached. The reading will be the same either way. If the coil is OK it should read some resistance, typically 400 - 700 ohms. Infinite resistance, no connection, may indicate a bad coil.

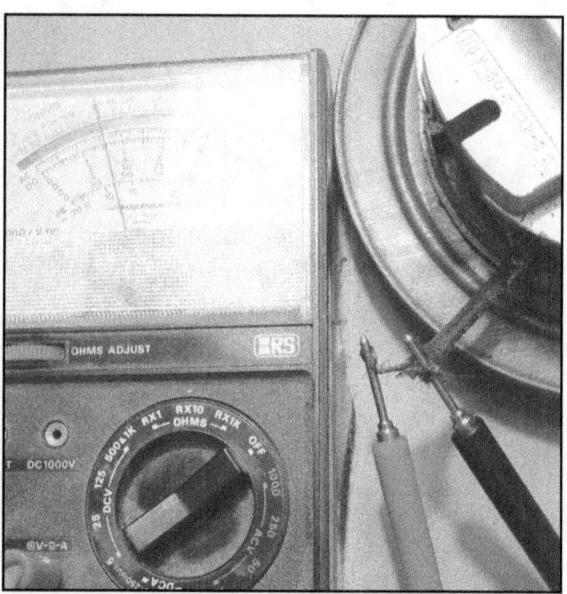

2. The Field and Coil

This paper wrapped coil supplies the magnetic field power to the stack of metal plates which in turn drive the rotor. The stack of metal plates are attached to the back plate with 3 - 5/16" nuts. Notice the specially shaped screw heads on the back of the motor. Use a flat blade screwdriver to hold them if needed while loosening the nuts. Other styles of motor may have a smooth head capscrew. On those, the head fits into a keyed hole in the case, so all you need to do is loosen the nut from the inside. Lift the field and coil assembly away from the back plate.

3. Mark the coil

Place a mark using a felt tip pen on the left hand side, top left corner, of the coil looking from the back. This mark will enable you to keep the exact same orientation of the coil to the field after you have replaced the cord. After making this mark you are ready to remove the metal plates. The side where you place this mark is also the same side where the old cord enters the coil wrapping and where your new cord will also enter the coil wrapping.

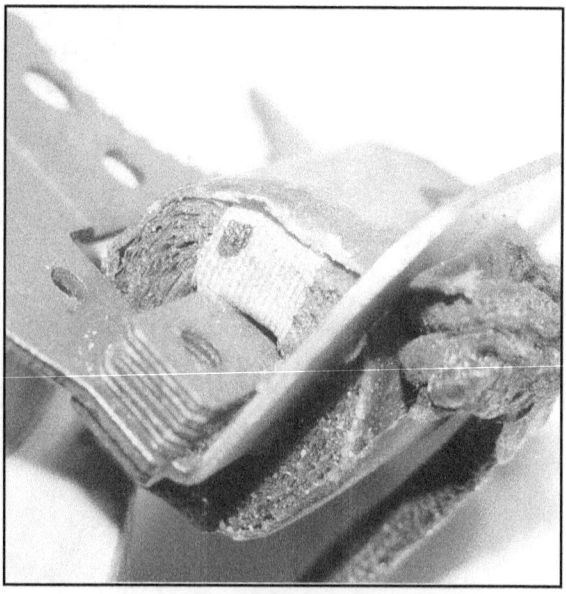

4. Remove the Field and Core

Slide the plates apart and remove them from the center of the coil. You will notice that the core is composed of a stack of metal plates. Keep these plates in the same orientation as they were while inside the coil. The field plates are at the bottom of the stack, one over the other. The field and core assembly is usually as follows: 7 or 8 plates on top, then the left side of the field, then the right side of the field at the bottom. Carefully set these plates aside and move on to removing the old power cord.

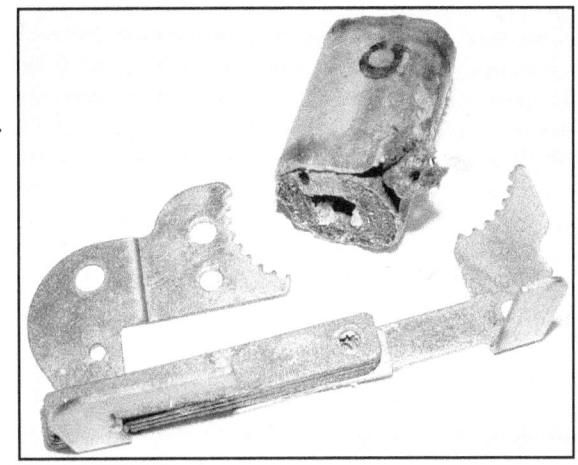

5. Open the Paper Wrapping

First, snip off the old cord as close to the coil as possible as shown here. Now with a sharp blade, carefully slice the paper covering directly over the old cord. The cord extends under the paper nearly the full width of the coil. You will be able to discern the lump of the wire under the paper. Carefully cut the paper and peel it back, layer by layer, to expose the wiring as shown in the next frame. Do not cut too deeply, you only want to separate the outer layer of paper.

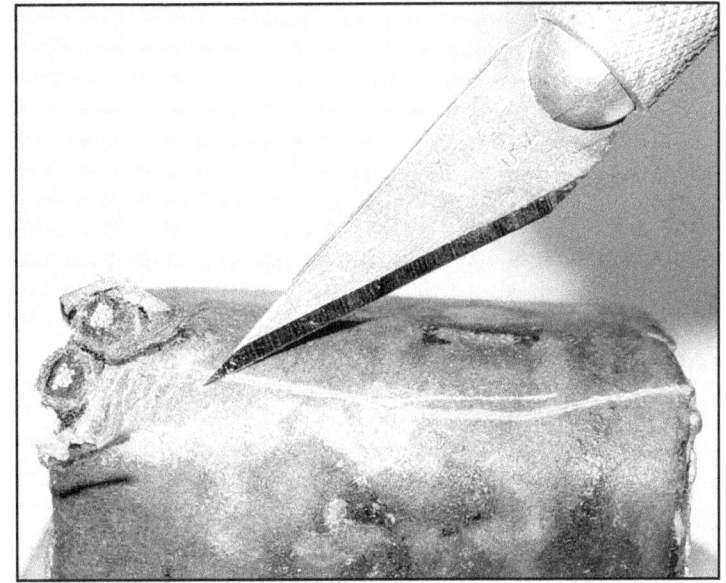

6. Expose the Leads

After cutting the paper and folding it back, slice off the two paper flaps from either side to clean up. See the tinned ends of the old cord, folded back as originally installed, with the magnet wire leads from the coil firmly soldered in place. Your objective now is to salvage the longest possible length of each magnet wire lead, snipping it closely to the point where it is soldered to the power cord. You will want to unbend the old power cord leads and unwind the magnet wire from the old power cord leads as far as possible, until the old solder joint prevents you from getting any more magnet wire.

7 Trim the Magnet Wire

Go ahead and slice the paper holding the old insulated cord to the coil. Unbend the leads and unwind the magnet wire from the old cord leads until you reach the point where it is soldered. Now carefully clip the magnet wire away from the old power cord at the solder joint. You may now remove the excess paper that was holding down the old wire.

8 Ready for new cord

What we end up with is a paper wrapped coil with two magnet wire leads coming out of the paper wrap. Do not cut away any more of this paper wrap than absolutely necessary. The wrap holds the coil together and provides insulation. Your goal at this time is to avoid sharply bending or needlessly flexing the magnet wire leads. Should it break off, you can unwrap the paper and try to unwind more wire, but this is difficult and may ruin the coil. Have a piece of tape handy to hold the windings if you try to unwrap the coil any farther.

9 A not so clean example

The previous examples show a clean, easy to work on coil. In this case the paper was brittle so the first slice went all the way down to between the old cord wires. The old rubber insulation has crumbled into a black gravely mess. You can see the leads on either side, but they were covered by rotten paper after my first cut, so I had to carefully strip the paper layers to uncover the leads and magnet wire. This will clean up OK and be just fine after removing the bits of rotten insulation and paper, straightening the leads and salvaging as much of the magnet wire leads as possible.

10 Messy coil after cleanup

The coil from frame 9, with rotten paper cut away and leads exposed, ready to clip the magnet wire at the solder joint. These two pictures are just to let you know that even if your coil appears to be in bad shape, it is salvageable, given that it is good in the first place. Now let's prepare the new cord to be installed on the coil.

11 Prepare the New Cord

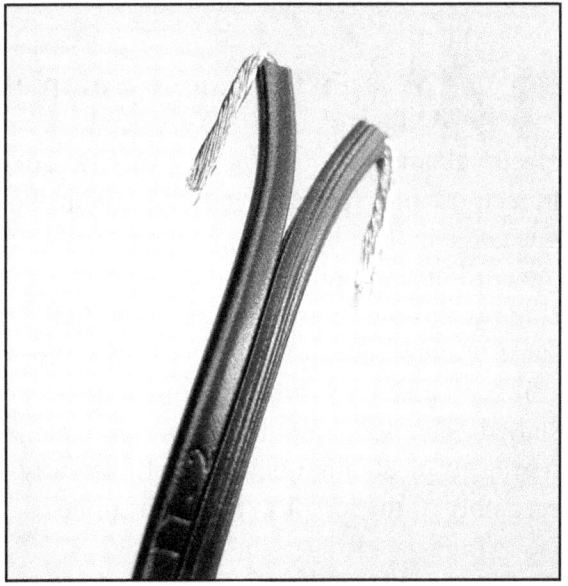

Select a 10ft. length of 18/2 lamp cord, available at most home centers. You can also get this cord with a plug attached in a lamp rewiring kit, although it will only be about six feet long. Strip about one half an inch of insulation at the end and bend the leads back as shown. You may be tempted to simply cut the end off an extension cord and use that with plug already attached. Don't. The extension cord is too thick, you will have problems fitting the coil into the motor and fitting the cord bushing will be impossible. If the cord you select already has a plug attached, slide the cord bushing on now. (See step 14)

12 Support the Coil

Wrap the coil to cover any exposed magnet wire windings, then place the coil into a vise to hold it steady while you attach the new cord.

13. Make connections and Solder

Lay the new cord across the coil in the same orientation as the original cord. Use the mark you placed on the coil in step 3 as a guide. After positioning the cord, apply 1 or 2 turns of tape to secure the cord against the coil. Attach each magnet wire lead to the new cord. Use tweezers or hemostat type pliers to manage the fine wires. Solder your connections. Heat the heavy connection area of the wire with the soldering iron from underneath. When the solder melts on touching the wire it's hot enough. Let the solder melt through from the top and coat the entire connection with solder for each side. It does not matter which side is positive.

14. Wrap with Tape to Complete

After soldering the connections, wrap the coil in electrical tape. Do not wrap too heavily, 2 or 3 turns is sufficient. It will be easier if you obtain wide black tape, about one and a half inches wide, and trim it slightly to fit. Install the cord bushing now if you have not done so already, flat side toward the motor. Assemble the field and core in the same orientation as original. You now have the completed core, coil and field with new cord attached and bushing installed as shown. You may re-use the vintage plug on your new cord or obtain a new plug. Either way, wait until re-assembly of the motor to install the plug.

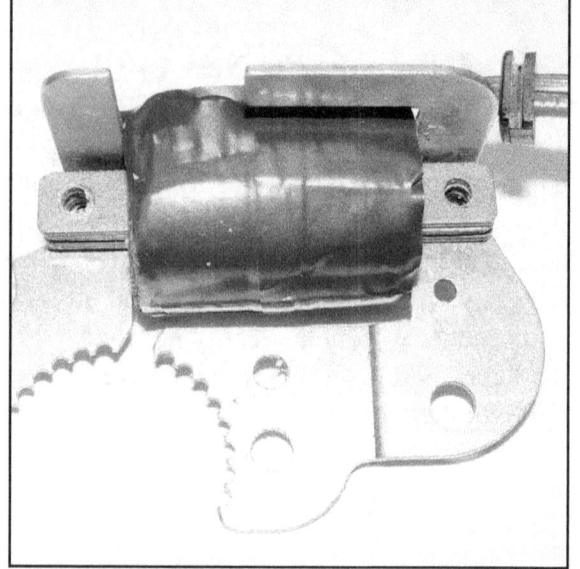

15. Summary

Congratulations! You have now replaced that old rotten power cord with a new, safer connection. Three discussion points: 1. The most tricky thing about this procedure is removing the old cord without damaging the magnet wire leads. Just be careful and go slowly when it is difficult to see where things are located due to decaying insulation. 2. When checking the coil with the ohm-meter, what you are looking for is some resistance, the number of ohms isn't critical but is usually between 400 - 700. If you read infinite resistance, indicating no connection at all, the coil is most likely bad and will require replacement. 3. The coil from any Hammond motored clock will work as a replacement, keeping in mind that the arrangement of the lead wires on the coil may be different and may require you to insulate or re-make the coil connection.

Chapter 4
Cleaning the Open Rotor Movement

1. Cleaning the Case
2. Cleaning the Dial
3. General Cleaning of the Gears
4. Cleaning the Rotor
5. Cleaning the Fiber Gear
6. Cleaning the Minute/Sec Gears
7. Cleaning the Plates
8. Summary

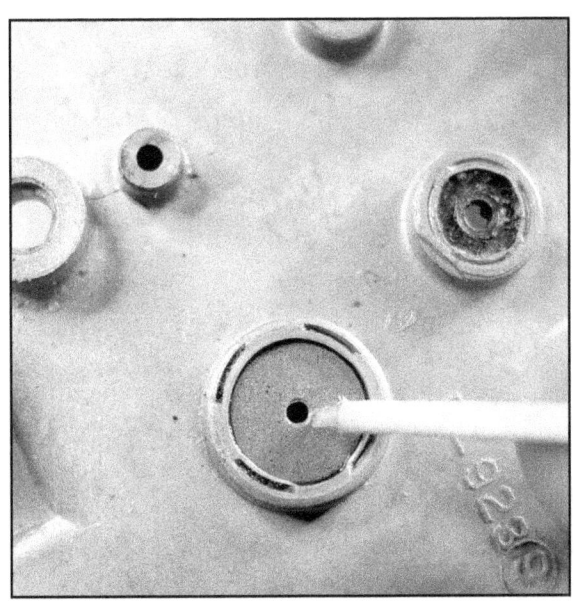

1 Cleaning the Case

The case for the Hammond Postal Telegraph is made from stamped steel. The original finish is black baked on enamel. The bezel ring is also stamped steel, with a chrome or nickel finish. If you are interested in plating your clock in copper, chrome or other alternative finishes, bear in mind that the condition of the surface has a great deal to do with the look of the finished product. Rusted or pitted metal must be cleaned and polished smooth prior to plating or it will ruin the new finish. Mild soap and water can be used to clean the painted surfaces. Be careful with polish on the bezel ring as the plated finish is not very thick.

2 Cleaning the Dial

The Postal Telegraph dial is paint on a metal dial pan. I do not recommend cleaning the dial. Besides, incidental water damage and aging give a clock face desirable character. If you feel that you must do something in the way of dial cleaning here are some tips. NEVER wipe the dial to clean it. Doing so will only smear the paint. Use dry compressed air to blow away some of the dust or a very soft brush to dislodge dust specks IF the paint is not flaking or cracked. If your dial is severely damaged, a professional clock dial painting and restoration service can make it look new again. If you do have the dial repainted and you would like to turn your clock into an unusual item, ask your dial painter about painting the numbers on in reverse order, with the 1 on the other side of the 12. Install this backwards dial and start your clock backwards for a real conversation piece! Hammond synchronous clocks will run just as well backwards as they do forwards. The author has one that has run backwards for many years with no problem.

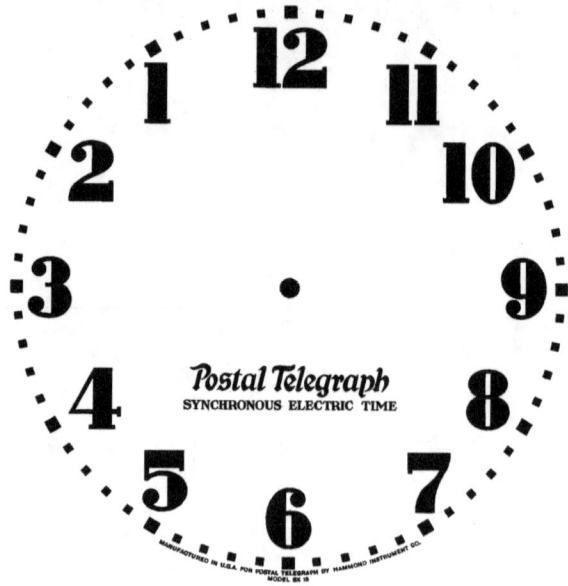

3 General Cleaning of the Gears

Manually cleaning the gears is a 5 step process. First loosen the dirt using oil, pithwood buttons and toothpicks or pegwood. Pithwood and pegwood are soft and easily absorb dirt and old oil while manually scrubbing the surface. Then string the parts on a wire and soak the wheels (except the fiber gear) in a clock cleaning solution. The solution can be simple as hot soapy water or a professional clock cleaning product. Anything that dissolves grease and doesn't harm brass will work. You may want to use a soft bristle brush on the parts after the first soaking, then soak them again. After soaking rinse in water, then rinse again in alcohol to remove moisture. Then dry the parts with hot air using a blow dryer or other forced air heat source.

If you are using a professional clock cleaning solution you can skip the manual cleaning and soak the parts for several hours or until they look clean. Follow the directions with the cleaner and **do the cleaning outside or with plenty of ventilation.**

4 Cleaning the Rotor

When cleaning the rotor, careful attention must be given to the torsion spring so as not to unhook it. If it does unhook, use tweezers to grasp the end of the spring and replace it between the pinion leaves. Clean the length of the brass pinion leaves with oil and a toothpick or pegwood. Make sure there isn't any built up where the weight contacts the steel rotor wheel at the bottom. Make sure the torsion spring is free of debris. You may use a razor blade to get in between the spring coils to loosen dried oil. Run the arbor ends into the pithwood button or use a towel to clean them.

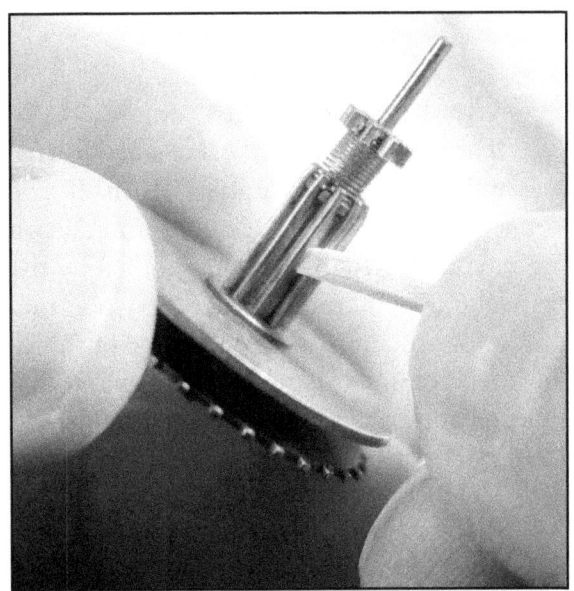

5 Cleaning the Fiber Gear

Use a rag and a little oil to gently clean the fiber gear. Be very careful here as this is gear can break. It is strong, but somewhat brittle. Run the teeth of the wheel lightly over the button pithwood and plunge the arbor ends into the pithwood to clean them. Finish by wiping the surface of the gear and the teeth with a little oil. Leaving a small amount of oil on this gear will help to preserve it and keep it from drying out. Avoid immersing this gear in any liquid.

6 Cleaning the Minute/Sec Gears

To clean inside the minute tube use a paper wire tie. Crumple the wire tie so that it will fit snugly into the tube, but loose enough that you can feed the tie through to the other end. Coat the wire tie with oil, then feed it through to the other end. Work the tie back and forth a few times, then extract. Clean any buildup of oil between the minute gear and the large pinion using a toothpick or pithwood to scrub between the pinion leaves while turning the pinion.

7 Cleaning the Plates

The clock plates are best cleaned by hand. Do not immerse the plates because it will be next to impossible for you to get the water and cleaning solution out of the bushing cavities. Clean the bushing holes by using sharpened pegwood or toothpicks. Insert the wood into the hole and turn it to scrub the inner edge of the bushing. You'll notice the stick getting dirty. Cut off the end, resharpen and continue cleaning the holes. A little oil can help with loosening the dirt. Be sure to remove any built up gunk on the surface of the bushing surrounding the hole.

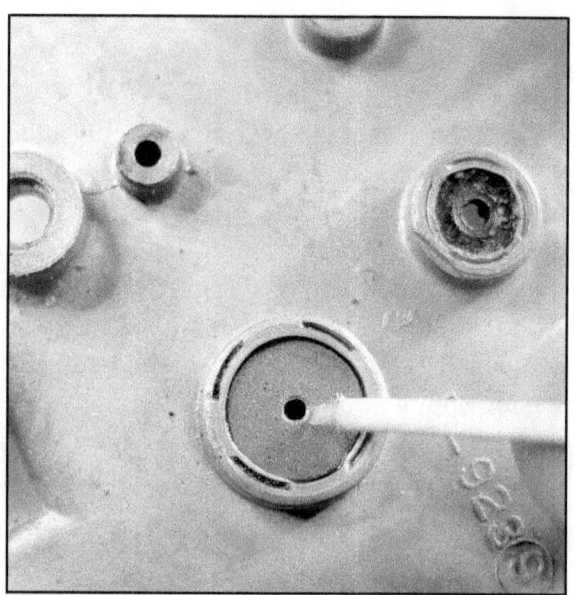

8 Summary

Getting all the dirt and dried oil out of the crevices of the gears will be nearly impossible without doing some kind of soaking in cleaning solution. The photos below show some Hammond clock gears before and after soaking in a professional clock cleaning solution. The solution was designed to be used in an ultrasonic cleaner, but it worked very well in removing most of the debris from these wheels. Even after soaking some of the thicker deposits may remain. Soak them again and manually try to get at as much of the debris as possible with your pegwood or toothpicks. After everything is clean you are ready to apply oil and re-assemble the motor.

Chapter 5
Oiling the Open Rotor Movement

1. Oiling the Rotor
2. Oiling the Set Gears - 1
3. Oiling the Set Gears - 2
4. Oiling the Set Gears - 3
5. Oiling the Minute Wheel and Pinion
6. Oiling the Minute Wheel Base
7. Oiling the Seconds Shaft
8. Oiling the Hour Wheel Base
9. Oiling the Hour Wheel Cannon
10. Oiling the Bushings - 1
11. Oiling the Bushings - 2
12. Oiling the Bushings - 3
13. Oiling the Bushings - 4
14. Oiling the Bushings - 5
15. Oiling the Bushings - 6
16. Oiling the Bushings - 7
17. Oiling the Bushings - 8

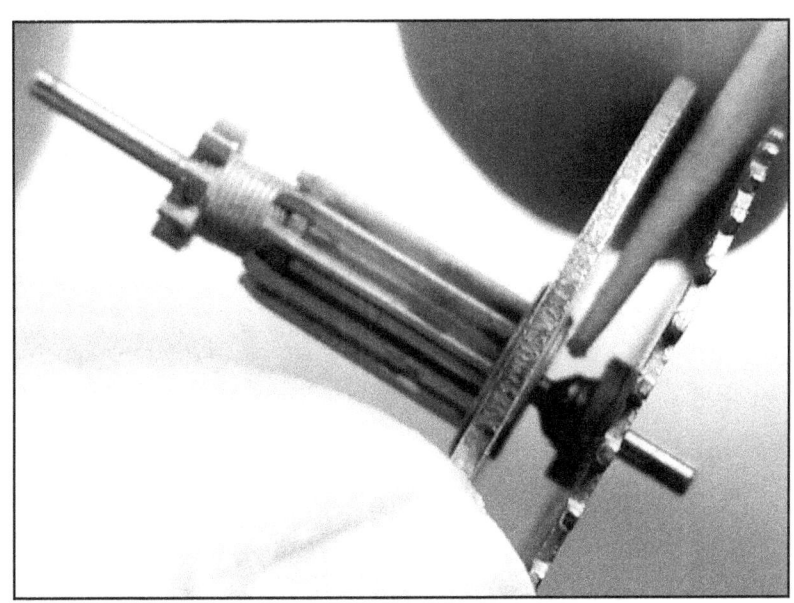

1 Oiling the Rotor

This is the main spot to oil the rotor, where the brass weight rides. As a rule, put as little oil as will do the job. More oil will just spread out over the wheels and cause a mess.

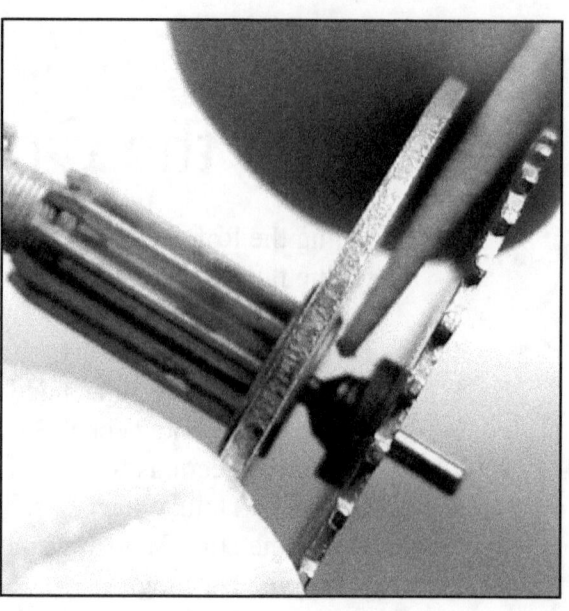

2 Oiling the Set Gears - A

Oil the set gears as shown in three places. First between the bottom two gears.

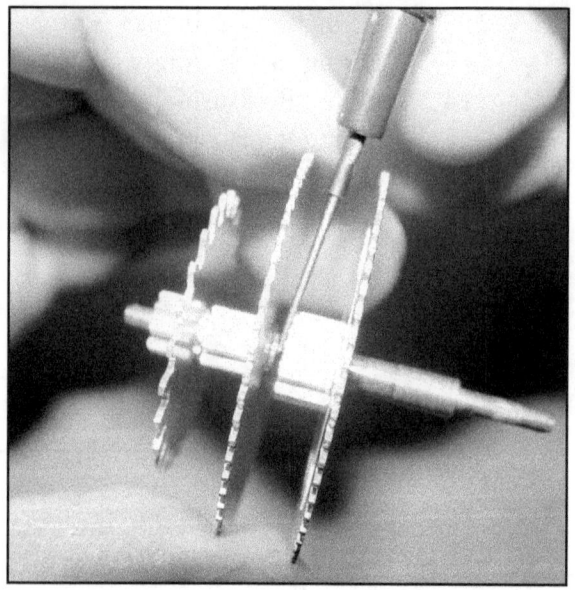

3 Oiling the Set Gears - B

Oil the set gears between the bottom gear and the spacer washer.

4. Oiling the Set Gears - C

Finally, oil the set gears between the top two gears. As a rule, do not put oil on the teeth of any wheel or pinion (a little on the fiber gear is OK). It will gather dust which will cause friction and wear on the pinion leaves.

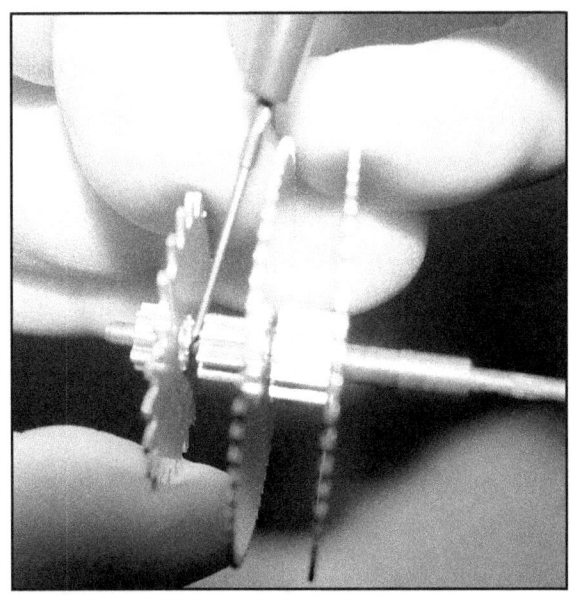

5. Oiling the Minute Wheel and Pinion

Put a drop of oil here between the minute pinion and wheel. Turn the pinion to spread the oil around and make sure it turns smoothly. This controls how smoothly the set knob will turn when you are setting the time so some extra time here making sure it turns smoothly will pay off later with a smooth feeling action.

6. Oiling the Minute Wheel Base

Put a drop of oil at the base of the minute wheel as shown. This surface rides on top of the seconds pinion. The seconds shaft rotates inside the minute tube.

7 Oiling the Seconds Shaft
Oil the surface of the seconds shaft. Notice the threaded end. Try not to get any oil on the threads.

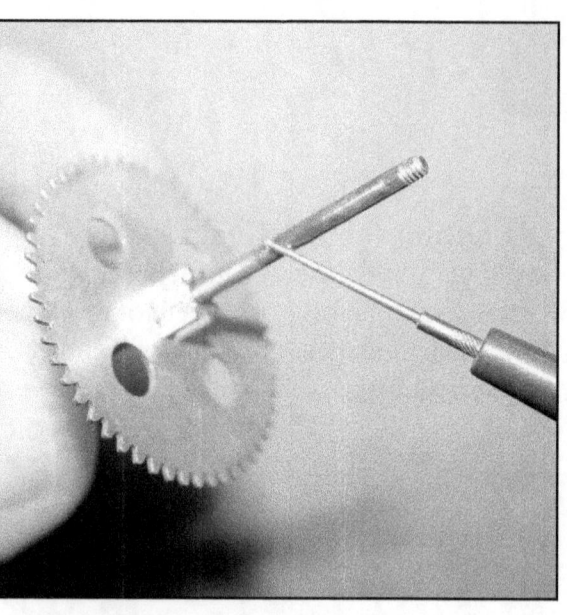

8 Oiling the Hour Wheel Base
Put a drop of oil on the inner edge of the hour wheel. This raised surface is where the minute wheel pinion will contact the hour wheel.

9 Oiling the Hour Wheel Cannon
Put a couple drops of oil inside the hour cannon so that the minute shaft will turn smoothly should it have contact. Spread it around a little bit to make sure the inner surface is lightly coated.

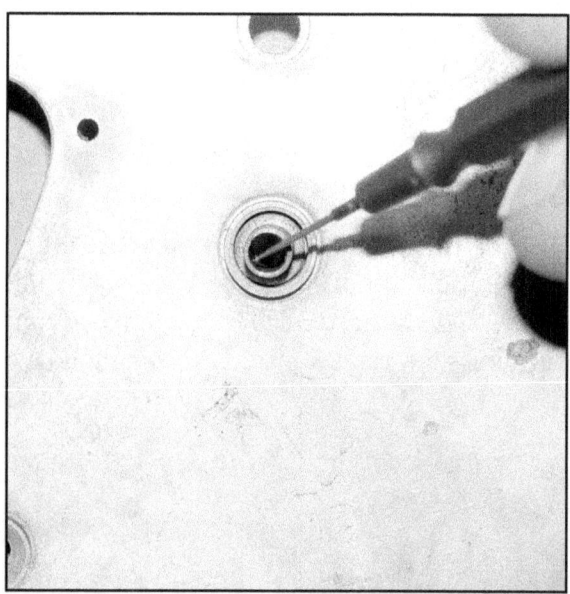

10 **Oiling the Bushings - A**
Oil the bushings, starting with the metal rotor bushing. Each bushing hole should get a drop of oil. If you put too much and the oil spreads out over the surface of the bushing wipe it off and try again.

11 **Oiling the Bushings - B**
Oil the start wheel bushing. Notice that this bushing is made of the same material as the start wheel. The rotor and start wheel bushings are the critical ones to have oiled right on the top plate.

12 **Oiling the Bushings - C**
Put some oil into the hole for the set wheels. It's not really a bushing, more of a hole in a raised nub on the plate.

13 **Oiling the Bushings - D**
On the back plate now, hit the four bushing holes with a drop of oil. Here is the rotor bushing being oiled.

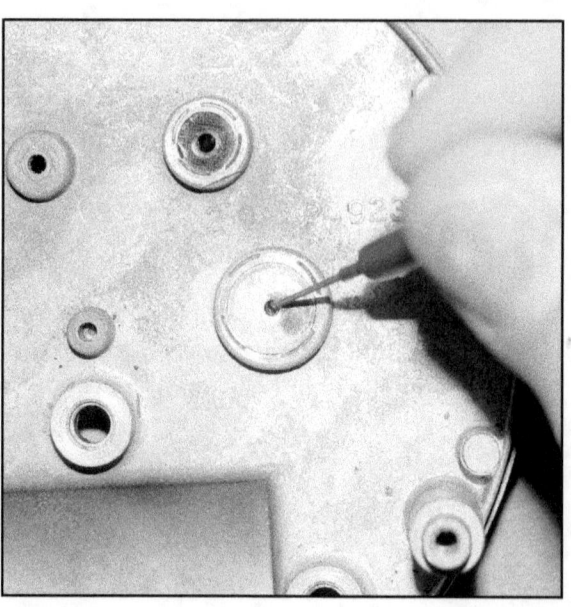

14 **Oiling the Bushings - E**
The start wheel bushing in the back plate goes all the way through for the start wheel knob. Some thicker oil, or just a little extra regular oil, on the surface of this bushing won't hurt. You may notice a worn area around the edge where the round washer on the start wheel contacts the bushing. This is the reason for a little extra oil here.

15 **Oiling the Bushings - F**
Oil the cast hole for the set gears. This one is open at the back for the set time knob.

16 Oiling the Bushings - G
And finally oil the cast hole for the minutes and seconds gears.

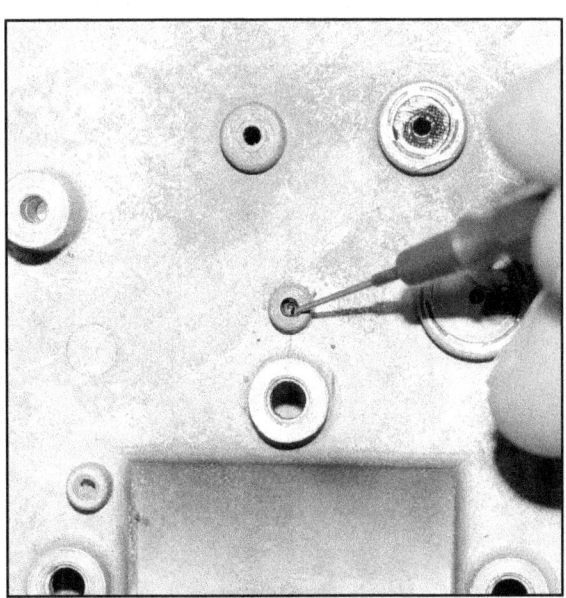

17 Oiling the Bushings - H
A little bit of oil from the back side of the back plate in both the set and start bushings and you are done oiling. Now prepare for assembly.

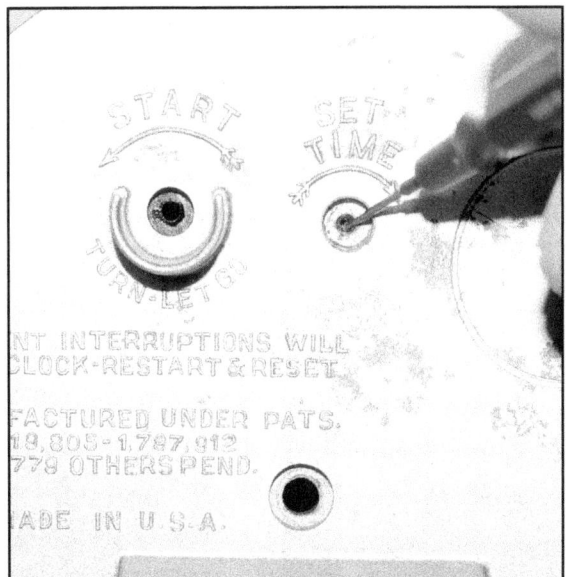

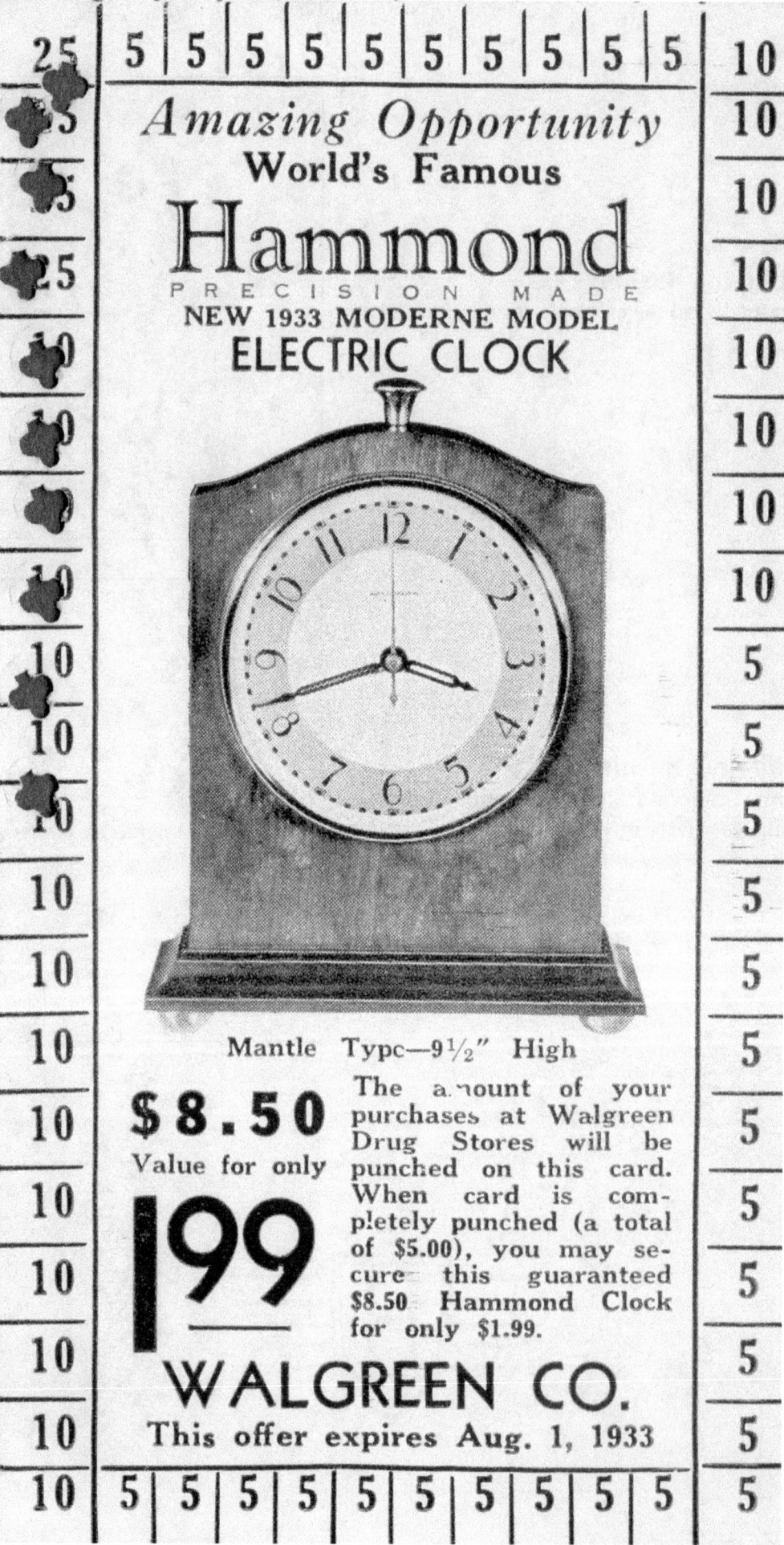

Chapter 6
Open Rotor Clock Assembly
Postal Telegraph SX15

1. Install the Field/Coil
2. Install the Rotor
3. Install the Start Wheel
4. Install the Set Gears
5. Install the Min/Sec Gears
6. Side View of Installed Gears
7. Install the Front Plate
8. Secure the Plates
9. Install the Motor and Knobs
10. Install the Dial
11. Install the Hands
12. Install the Glass
13. Install the Bezel Ring
14. Install the Backer Board
15. Assembly Complete

1. Install the Field/Coil

Now we can re-assemble Postal Telegraph clock. In general the assembly is the reverse of dis-assembly but there are some tricks and processes to follow to make a smooth job. As always, read all the steps and instructions before doing anything. First, attach the field and coil assembly to the back plate as shown. Use the three screws and 5/16" nuts. At this time, route your cord out of the case and through the bushing as shown in step 8.

2. Install the Rotor

After attaching the field and coil assembly, it's time to set the wheels into their bushings. First put the rotor into it's bushing.

3. Install the Start Wheel

Next, install the start wheel with the round spacer side down, contacting the bushing and allowing just the right amount to extend out to accept the start knob.

4 Install the Set Gears
Now put in the set gears, once again round spacer side down to allow the shaft to extend out the bushing hole for the set knob.

5 Install the Min/Sec Gears
Now install the minutes and seconds gear set. This one is a little tricky. Lift the set gears up a little and slip the min/sec gears in between and seat the shaft into it's bushing.

6 Side View of Installed Gears
Here is a side view of the completed clock motor. During assembly hold the motor up to eye level from time to time to make certain that the gears are meshing correctly.

7. Install the Front Plate

Now set the front plate on top of your motor and allow the min/sec shaft to go through the hour wheel. Remember that the oval shaped hole in the front plate goes over the coil. Lift the motor up to eye level and look inside. Each of the 3 shafts will be contacting the plate in the area of their bushing holes. Using your finger, nudge each wheel into it's bushing hole until all three are seated and the top plate drops into place.

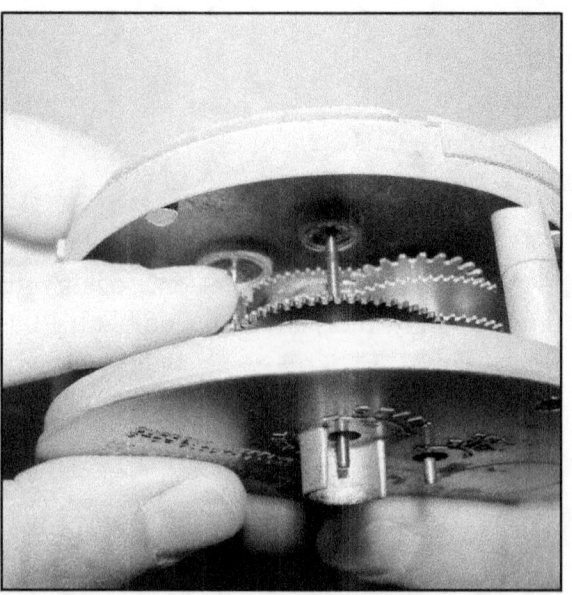

8. Secure the Plates

Attach the mounting flange with it's three screws. Now attend to the cord and make sure it is routed the way you want with the cord bushing in place in it's slot in the back plate. The example shows the cord routed around one of the motor mount posts. Install the motor dust cover then attach the motor to the case.

9. Install the Motor and Knobs

Attach the motor to the case via the three screws in the mounting flange then install the start and set knobs on the back of the motor. These knobs are friction fit and finger pressure should be plenty to install them. The smaller knob is the "start" knob.

10. Install the Dial

Now install the dial. Lay it in place with the 12 near the top of the case where the hanger is mounted. You will notice small holes in the dial at 6 and 12 and corresponding dimples in the case. These are for precise location of the dial pan. Now you are ready to install the hands.

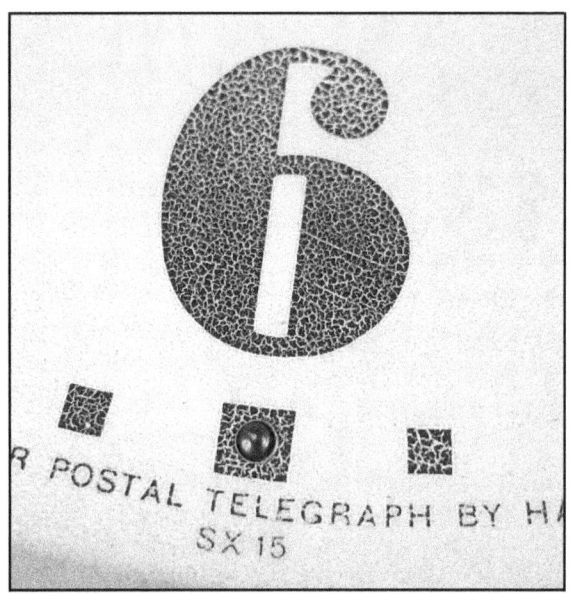

11. Install the Hands

Put the minute hand on first and align it to the 12 by turning the set knob. Now remove the minute hand and press the hour hand into place pointed directly at 3. This will make certain that your hands are properly aligned. Make sure the hour hand does not touch the dial by turning it through one full cycle. Adjust as needed. After the hour hand is installed, put the minute hand on again and install the small 7/32" nut to hold it in place. Check that the two hands do not touch one another during any part of their travel. Now hold the start knob and thread the second hand onto it's shaft clockwise. Check all three hands for alignment.

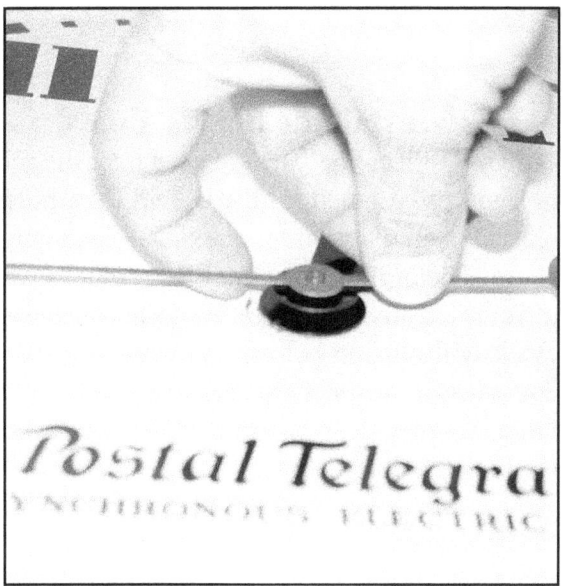

12. Install the Glass

Now lay the glass on top of the dial and check hand alignment again. You want to be certain that the second hand does not touch the glass. Also review the other hands alignment now. Slight bending of the hands can be done to improve alignment. Just remember that all 3 hands must revolve without interfering with the dial, glass or each other. Turn all the hands full circle several times to check. Looking from the edge with the clock tilted up can help identify any mis-alignment.

13 Install the Bezel Ring

With the glass in place and the hands aligned now put the bezel in place and work the tabs down into the slots located at approximately 12, 2, 4, 6, 8 and 10. When the bezel is down, gently turn the clock over onto it's face. Now twist the bezel tabs slightly to maintain friction and hold the bezel in place.

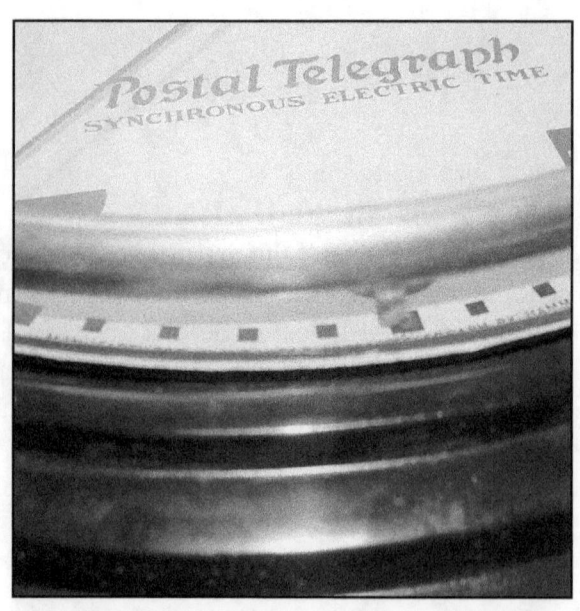

14 Install the Backer Board

Place the backer board over the motor and position the three holes to line up with the holes in the back plate. Watch that your cord exits at the notch in the backer board. The original design of these clocks was for the cord to route out the top and plug in above the clock. If your clock will plug in below, you may want to carve a notch down low in the backer board to allow the cord to route out there. You may also want to notch the case near the bottom to allow the cord access.

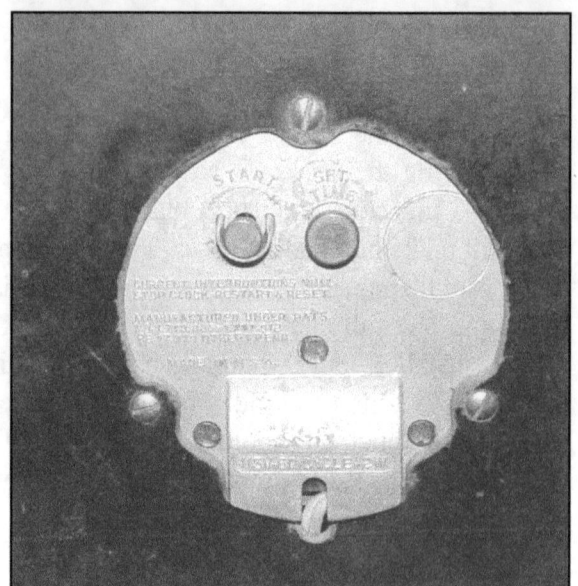

15 Assembly Complete

Job well done! Your clock is now cleaned and ready for service. Hang it up, give it a spin and watch it go!

Chapter 7
Disassembly and Re-assembly
"Gregory" Desk Clock with Calendar

1. The Gregory
2. Remove the Outer Case
3. Remove the Case Back
4. Remove the Sealed Rotor Unit
5. Remove the Hands
6. Remove the Dial
7. Separate the Plates
8. Remove the Wheels for Cleaning
9. Oiling the Minutes Gear
10. Assembling the Gear Train
11. Calendar Synchronization and Final Assembly
12. Polishing the Bakelite Case

Gregory

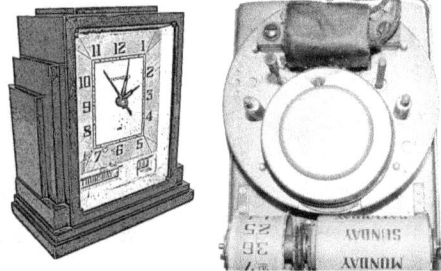

Sealed Rotor Movement

The fine details on cleaning and oiling have already been covered so I will not go into them here. Please refer to the earlier chapters on cleaning and oiling for detailed instructions.

Be advised: The Gregory clock is more difficult to reassemble than an Open Rotor type clock like the Postal Telegraph described in earlier chapters. I suggest you become proficient in assembly and disassembly of the Open Rotor type of movement in one of the many other desktop style clocks before getting into this project. This project does not cover disassembly of the calendar mechanism and we leave it whole during the processes in this chapter.

1 Introduction
There are two distinct styles of the Gregory model. One has a black Bakelite case with silver face and green second hand. The other has a brown Bakelite case with brown face and gold second hand. Internally they are identical and both employ the sealed rotor movement which is unlike the round open rotor movement we worked on in the Hammond Postal Telegraph clock. Let's open this clock and take a look.

2 Remove the Outer Case
Turn the clock over onto it's face on your bench, using a towel for cushion. First remove the set time knob. Hold the shaft of the knob with pliers while turning the knob counter clockwise to unthread. Then remove the 4 slotted screws holding the case. Now turn the clock face up and lift the Bakelite case away from the frame. Remove the glass plate. **If you need replacement glass, it measures 5³/₈" by 3¹⁵/₁₆", single strength thickness.**

3 Remove the Back Plate
Turn the clock frame onto it's face. Now remove the two 1/4" nuts holding the back plate and data plate. Set these items aside.

4. Remove the Sealed Rotor Unit

If there are any washers left from the back case remove them then remove the two 5/16" nuts on the rotor hold down bar. Now lift out the sealed rotor unit. It rests upon a paper cushion. Set the paper cushion and sealed rotor aside and proceed to disassemble the rest of the clock as outlined below. If you like you can stop now and work on the Sealed Rotor and come back to this section later.

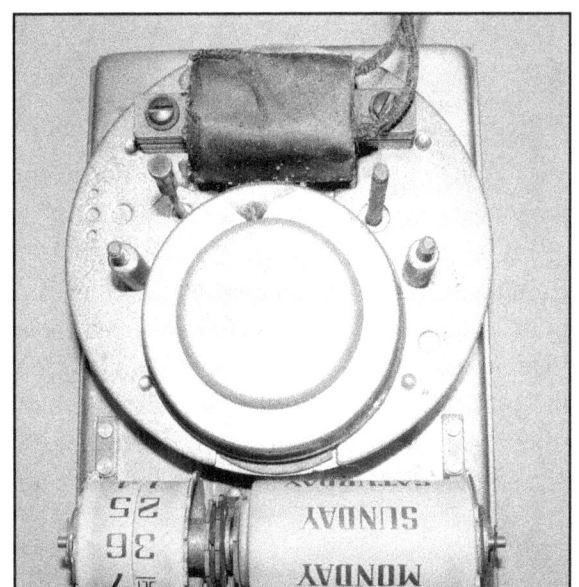

5. Remove the Hands

Start by removing the second hand. It is friction fit. Hold the start knob in back while turning the second hand counter clock wise. It should gradually loosen and come off. Remove the minute hand by loosening and removing the knurled nut holding it in place. The minute hand has a rectangular hole for correct alignment. The hour hand is friction fit and can be removed by pulling upwards at the center.

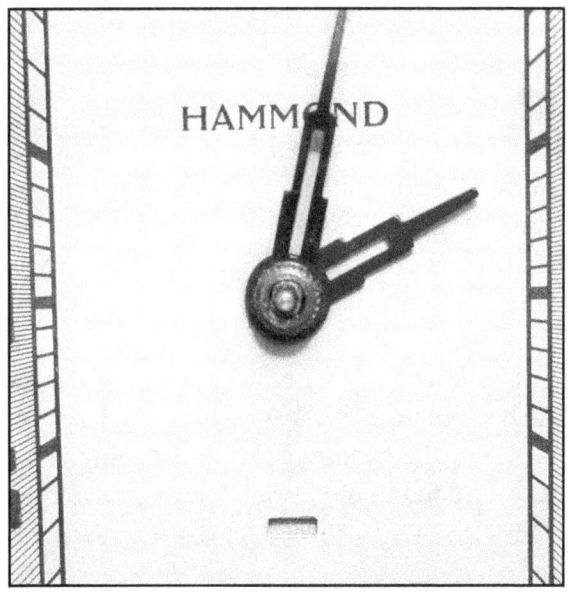

6. Remove the Dial

Remove the dial by bending down the tabs at each of the four corners. Try to bend just the minimum amount to free the dial pan. Use the end of a small flat blade screwdriver to work the tabs. The dial for this clock is painted metal and the numbers are embossed into the metal pan.

7. Separate the Plates

Once the dial is removed the four frame nuts holding the plates together are exposed. Use the 1/4" driver to loosen and remove these nuts. Now hold the back of the clock frame in one hand while holding the edge of the front round plate with the other hand. The front round plate is attached to and will come away with the calendar mechanism. Once the plates are apart set the calendar mechanism and front round plate assembly aside. We will not be disassembling it any farther. No oil will be applied to the calendar.

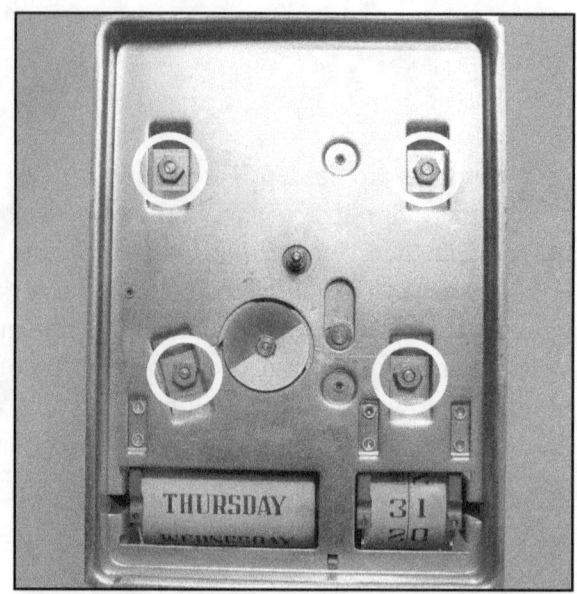

8. Remove the Wheels for Cleaning

Lift out the wheels one at a time for cleaning. Note the small spring location on the start wheel. Set the spring aside. Remove friction fit start knob by pulling it off the shaft with your fingers. It shouldn't be very tight. Now you can remove the start wheel from the back plate. What we have now is the back plate with field and coil assembly. At this time you can replace the cord if needed and clean the back plate as well as the wheels. Use your pegwood to clean out the bushings and do cleaning similar to the process outlined in the Postal Telegraph section of this book.

9. Oiling

When oiling, pay particular attention to the minutes gear shown here. The friction between the wide flat pinion at the base and the outer wheel will determine how easy or difficult setting the time will be. If there is not sufficient lubrication here, the set time knob will be stiff and jumpy. Take some time here to apply a little more oil between the base pinion and the gear. Work it by holding the minute hand shaft in a pliers while turning the outer gear.

Pinion

10 Assembly

After cleaning and oiling, you are ready to assemble. Pay particular attention to the minute wheel and pinion (has flat triangular spring) as this controls how smoothly the set knob will turn. Once the wheels are placed, remove the brass dust shield and position the front round plate and calendar assembly over the top and begin nudging the gears into their bushings. Take care, the flat gears tend to bind on one another. Take your time while positioning the arbors. Turn the gears slightly if they bind. Once everything is seated install the 4 frame nuts to secure the plates. Be careful to hold the frame steady while installing the 4 frame nuts. Have patience and take your time.

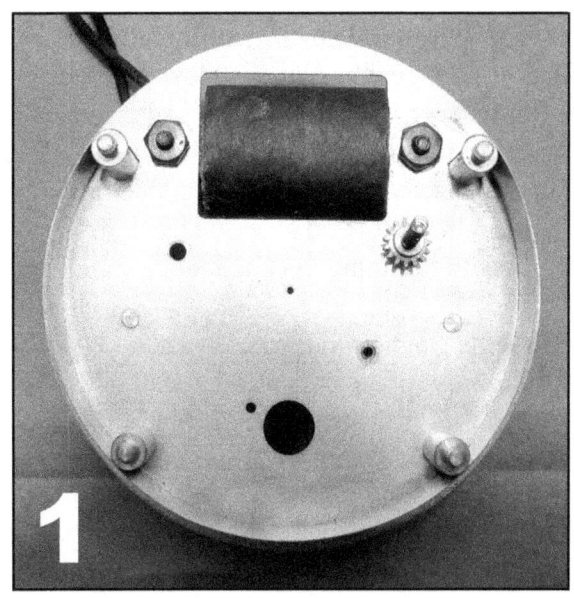

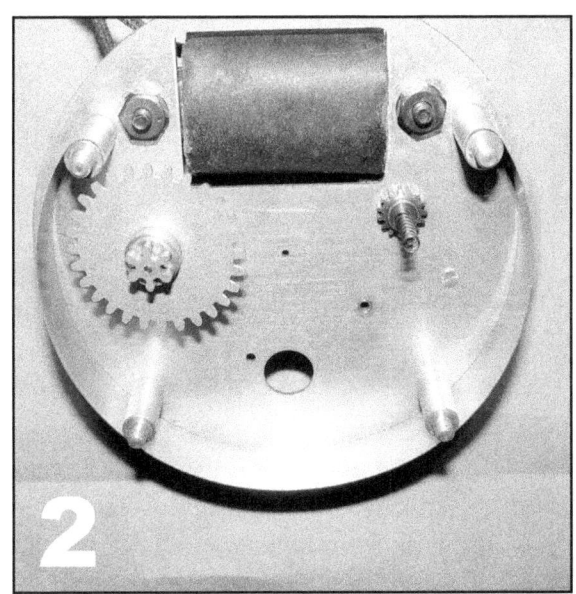

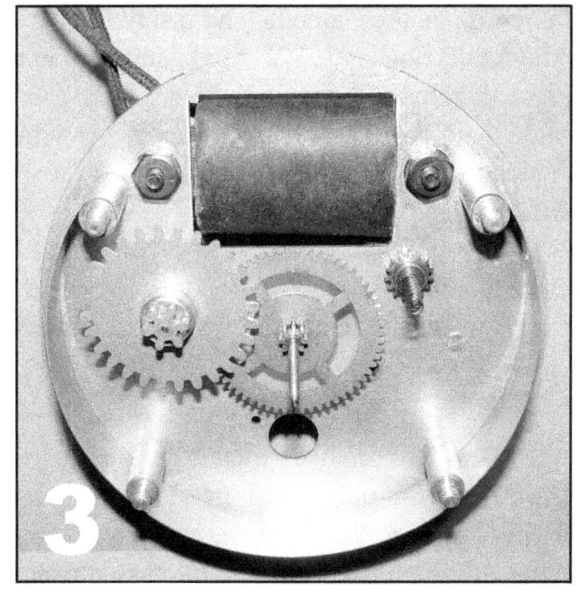

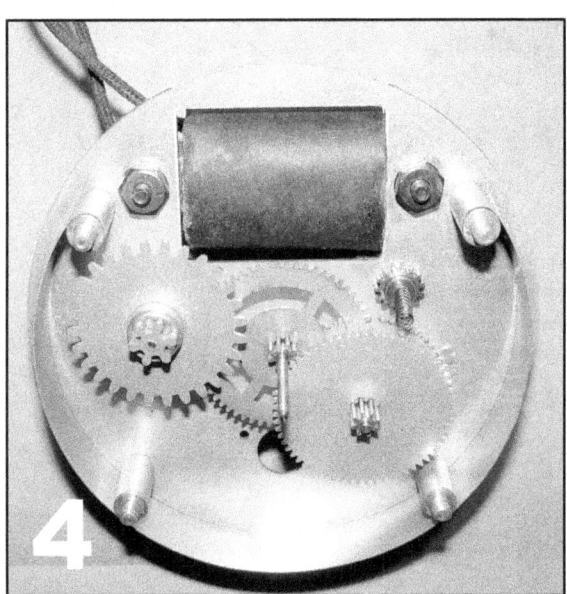

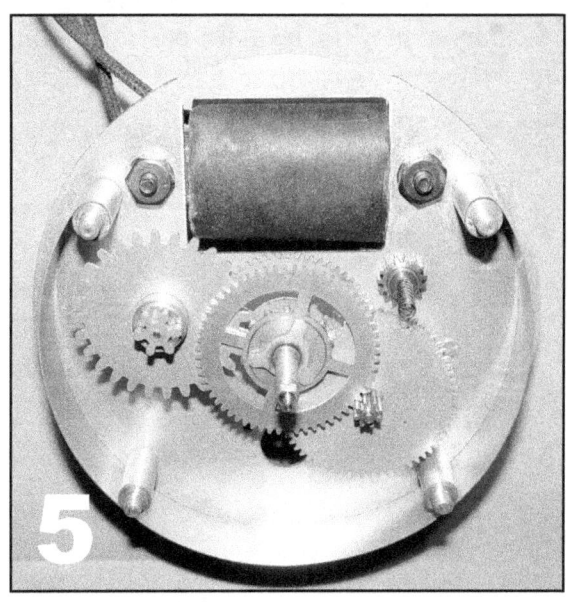

11 Final Assembly and Calendar Synchronization

Once the plates are fastened together you can install the dial, hands and synchronize the calendar. After installing the dial, temporarily install the set time knob. Turn the knob forward until the day and date make a full cycle. Just when the day and date have fully changed over, stop turning. Now set the minute hand in place and turn the set knob either forward or backward until the hand is aligned at 12. Now install the hour hand pointed at 2. You have just synchronized the clock and it is now set for 2am. The day and date will begin changing over at about midnight as I believe was the factory intent for this display.

Place the gears onto the back plate
Fit the front plate and calendar frame over the gears
Attach the 4 nuts to fasten the plates together
Install the brass dust cover around the gear train
Install the paper washer, sealed rotor unit and rotor keeper & nuts
Fit the start knob back onto it's arbor if you removed it
Install the Dial, bending the tabs just enough to hold it in place
Temporarily install the set knob
Synchronize the Calendar and install the hands - remove the set knob
Attach the clock case back and data plate with the 2 retaining nuts
Place the glass down into the clock case
Slide the clock frame down into the case without binding the cord
Attach the clock frame to the case with the 4 slotted screws
Attach the set knob

Once again, fitting the front plate and calendar assembly over the assembled back plate and gear train is not easy. Take your time and make sure everything is lined up.

12 Polishing the Bakelite Case

You can use a metal type polish to polish the Bakelite case. I have used MOTHERS brand Mag and Aluminum polish with good effect. I first washed the case in the sink with warm soapy water. After drying I applied the polish using a circular motion. The cloth will turn dark from polishing but this is OK. After rubbing it in for a little bit, take a clean towel and buff it off. Try this on a hidden area of your case before doing the front or sides because age and conditions can have different effects on Bakelite and your case may or may not be in the best condition for this kind of polishing.

Chapter 8
Sealed Rotor Treatment

1. Sealed Rotor Unit
2. Opening the Seal
3. Pry up the Stopper
4. Treatment for Dried Oil
5. Clean up and Reseal

Opening the Rotor
1. Soak and Clean
2. Oiling
3. Reassembly

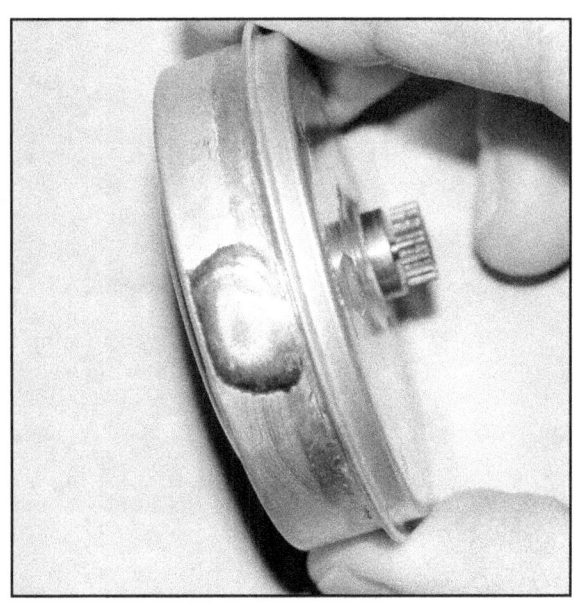

1. Sealed Rotor Unit

Here is the sealed rotor that is common in many early Hammond clocks. It is a sealed unit and designed by Hammond to be permanently oiled and never opened again. The problem is usually that the old oil has dried up. We will investigate two different approaches for getting these to work again. Our first approach will be to remove the solder blob, unplug the unit, dilute and drain as much of the old lube as possible, re-oil and reseal. The second approach will be to completely open the unit, clean it, oil it and then reinstall the unit as an unsealed, open rotor.

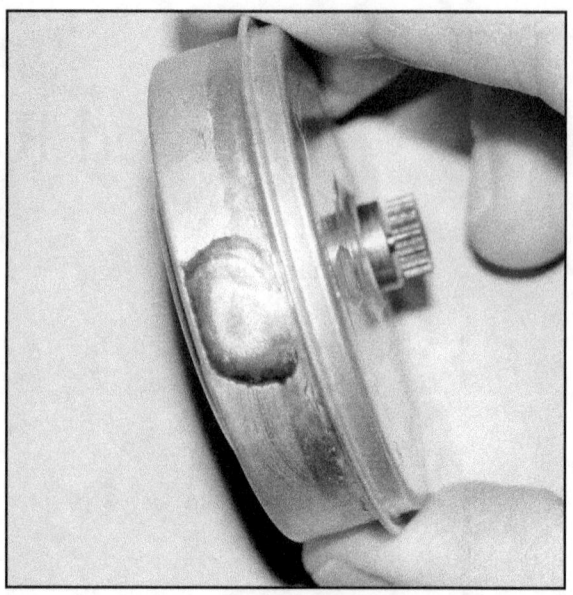

2. Opening the Seal

In this first approach to reviving the failed sealed rotor unit we will open the original oil plug by removing the solder seal from the case. Support the unit as shown in a vise. Apply heat from a propane torch, such as a Bernz-O-Matic from the home center. Position the unit so the solder runs down and away. Using a rag, wipe off as much of the solder as possible while it is hot.

3. Pry up the Stopper

Now that the solder is removed, use a small screwdriver to get up under the edge of the brass plug which covers the original oil hole. Go around the edge and gradually pry out the stopper.

4. Treatment for Dried Oil

First, fill the unit with penetrating oil, similar to Liquid Wrench or 3-IN-ONE Penetrating oil. You may need to sharpen the plastic nozzle of the squeeze bottle with a razor until it just fits into the oil port. This will be messy, so be prepared with towels or newspapers and a suitable work area. Squeeze the can or plastic bottle to fill the sealed rotor unit. Fill it up about half way, then shake it for a while, then fill it up the rest of the way. After it's full, work the output gears for a while (if it isn't frozen) and then let it sit, full of penetrating oil, for 24 hours. This will start to dissolve some of the old oil. Try to turn the output gear. If it is still frozen let it soak longer then try it again. You may also use pliers to gently break it loose if your fingers can't grip it well enough to turn.

After soaking in penetrating oil for at least 24 hours, drain by shaking out as much as possible while spinning the output gear. The oil coming out will be green and may contain solid chunks of dried lubricant. Now fill the unit again, this time with plain 3-IN-ONE oil. Clock oil could be used but is rather expensive to just throw away as we are doing here. Again, sharpen the plastic nozzle of the squeeze bottle until it just fits into the oil port, and squeeze to fill the rotor with 3-IN-ONE oil. Work the output gear. Let it sit full of the new oil for another 24 hours. Now drain it, first by shaking it out as much as possible and spinning the output. Then leave it to drain on some towels or newspaper for at least 24 hours. The oil coming out will still be green but don't worry about it. It's next to impossible to get all the old oil out of the rotor without complete disassembly, nor is that really required. This process is to soften any hardened oil, dilute the old oil and add in some fresh lubricant.

After fully draining, test the unit by spinning the output gear. From a fairly hard spin it should freewheel for about 20 seconds if it's ready. No other oil or treatment is required. There is still plenty of the old oil mixed with 3-IN-ONE inside this rotor.

If the output gear is still frozen after this treatment go to step 6 in this chapter where I describe completely opening the sealed unit for complete degreasing and oiling.

5. Clean up and Reseal

After lubrication and draining, clean the outside of the unit with rubbing alcohol to remove any traces of oil. Now to reseal the unit, I suggest that you cover the oil hole with metallic aluminum tape. This will save you the trouble of unsoldering the plug the next time the unit needs re-oiling. Now simply reinstall the unit in the clock and it's ready to go. If your rotor needs a more invasive procedure to get it going, proceed to step 6 where we begin disassembly of this sealed unit.

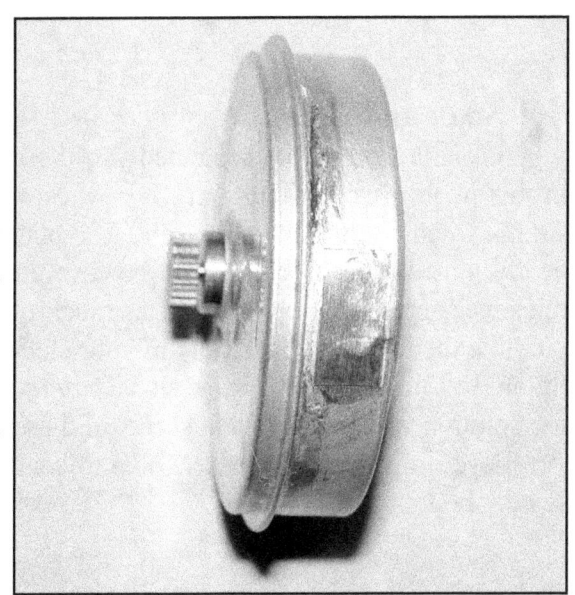

Opening the Rotor
This is an extreme approach and is only to be done as a very last resort. Do not do this unless you have tried the non-invasive repairs shown in previous steps. After removing the solder blob, heat the edge of the unit to soften the solder bead around the circumference of the unit and wipe off as much solder as possible. Then you'll see a lip where the two halves are joined, bottom edge rolled over the top (bottom being the gear side). Support the unit in a vise, gear side down as shown in the photo and go around the edge with a small sharp screwdriver bending the lip up to release the top half. Pry up the larger half and lift it off.

1 Soak and Clean
Once the halves are separated you'll see the inside as in this photo. Inside there is a rotor wheel and fiber gear similar to an open rotor movement. The plates are permanently joined. This assembly will be covered in a slime of thickened, greenish oil. Wipe off as much of this gunk as possible then soak the assembly in your clock cleaning solution. Nothing short of a professional strength clock cleaning solution will get all of that slime off these parts. Unless you have an ultrasonic cleaner, plan to soak this unit for several hours.

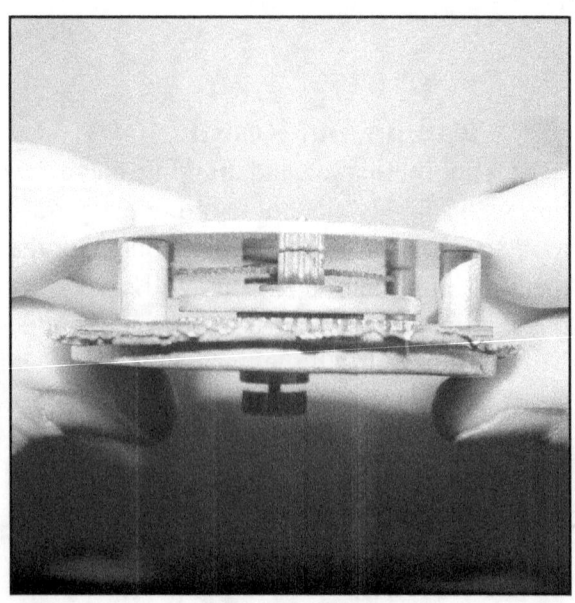

2. Oiling

Oiling this unit is a little difficult since the plates are riveted together and are not separable. It's easy to see the two holes for the gears in the back plate. Notice that these holes aren't equipped with any kind of oil sink around the edge, so you will need to make sure they are well oiled. You may want to experiment with some thicker oil or grease at the bearing points since this unit was designed to operate sealed in grease. To oil the bottom bushings try using a long nose, bent tip oiler. It is difficult to see the exact oiling points inside so feel your way with the tip of the oiler to find the bushing point.

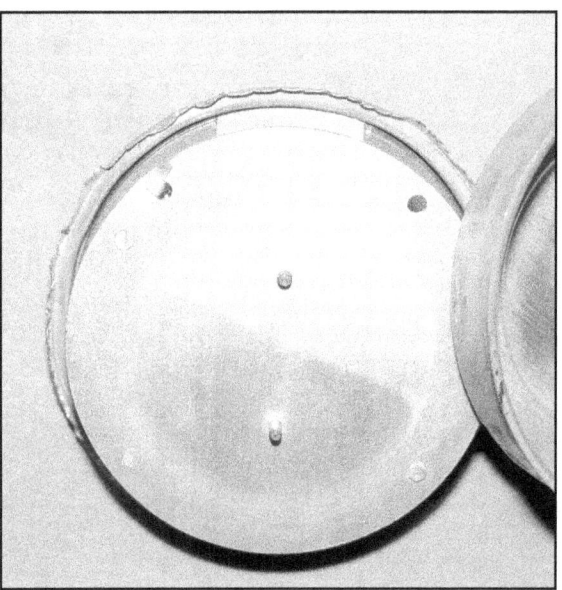

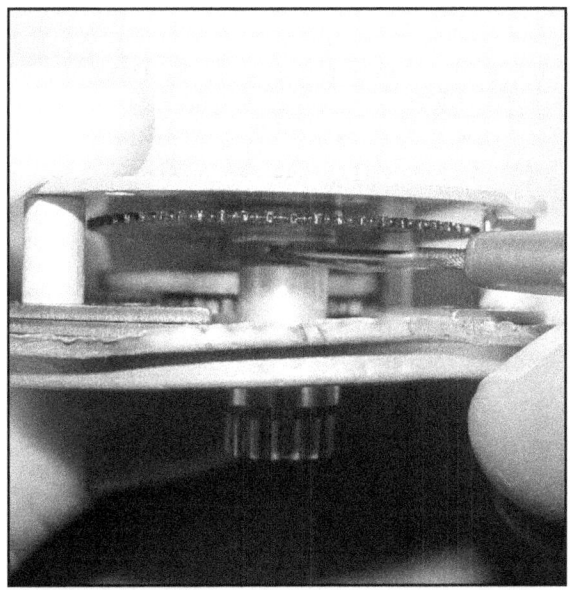

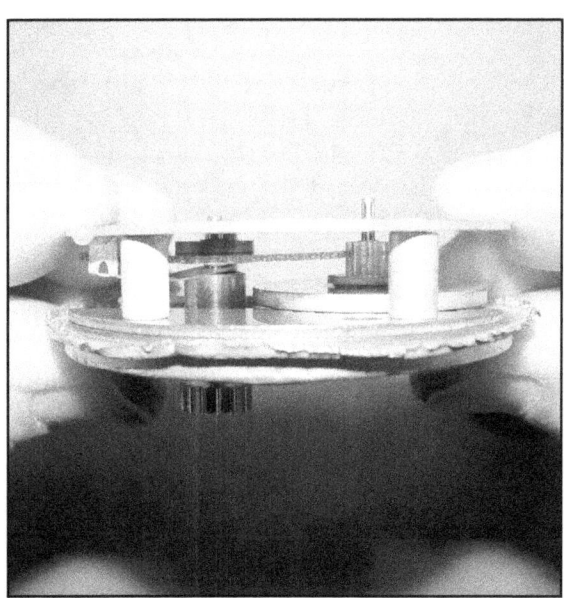

3. Reassembly

After everything is oiled to your satisfaction and the unit will freewheel for about 20 seconds following a good spin, snap the two halves together. Make sure the hole is away from the gear as original. If you like you can smooth out the rough edge left from opening the case by trimming, grinding or filing. Replace the unit into the clock in it's original location. It may be a tight fit against the posts now that the edge of the case is a little wider. Just snap it down into place, making sure that the start knob will spin the rotor, reassemble the clock and it's ready to go. Keep in mind that since this unit was designed to run in a bath of grease, you may want to try different or thicker oils to obtain the best running performance.

GUARANTEE

This electric clock movement is fully guaranteed by The Hammond Clock Company, Chicago, subject to the following conditions:

Any part or parts proving defective within one year from date of purchase will be replaced or repaired without expense to the customer other than transportation charges.

This guarantee does not apply to any movement used on a current supply different from that indicated on the name plate of the clock. Any evidence of tampering with the movement will be sufficient cause to invalidate the guarantee. To make this guarantee effective and to establish the duration of the guarantee period, a record of your purchase must be filed with The Hammond Clock Company. To do this, fill out the other part of this card and mail it at once. If the card is not mailed to The Hammond Clock Company, the factory record for the guarantee period will govern the expiration date of the free replacement period.

SERVICE

If you have reason to think that your clock is not operating properly, return it to the local dealer who can repair it for you or write direct to the Service Department of The Hammond Clock Company, Chicago, Illinois, for instructions and advice. Describe the difficulty as fully as possible and DO NOT return the clock before writing, as the necessity for doing so can usually be eliminated.

NOTICE

This clock movement is equipped with a Hammond Type "C" synchronous electric clock motor which is detachable. The motor unit is sealed in a container and runs in oil. This type of construction assures a long period of satisfactory service and eliminates the need for attention or oiling.

If the motor should ever wear out or require service, your clock can be given an entirely new span of life by merely replacing the motor. Your local dealer can install a new motor for a small charge or you may obtain full instructions from The Hammond Clock Company.

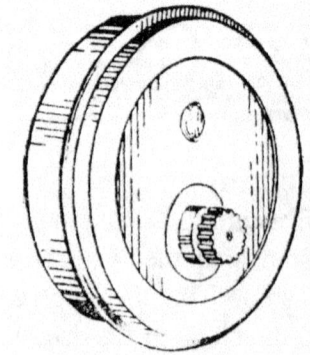

Type C Motor

YOUR RECORD

Guarantee Card mailed..............................
                                             (date)

Serial No..........................

Form KG

Bibliography

In my study of Hammond clocks and of electric clocks in general, I've found several books and articles which the reader may find of interest.

150 Years of Electric Horology 1992 NAWCC Chicago National Convention Exhibit edited by Elmer G. Crum & William F. Keller 1992 Midwest Electric Horology Group

Advertising Clocks by Michael Bruner 1995 Schiffer Publishing LTD

The Best of J.E. Coleman: Clockmaker by Orville R. Hagans 1979 American Watchmakers Institute Press

The Clock Repair Primer by Philip E. Balcomb 1986 Tempus Press

Electrifying Time: Telechron & G.E. Clocks, 1925 - 1955 by Jim Linz 2001 Schiffer Publishing LTD

The National Association of Watch and Clock Collectors, Inc. NAWCC Bulletin Volume 43/2 No. 331 Page 167 - 176 "Clocks Were Not the Only Thing" by William F. Keller 2001 NAWCC

Spin to Start Journal of the Synchronous Society Hammond Clock Collectors International Volume 1, No. 1 1996 Edited by Allen R. Miller

Hammond Ephemera

54   Punch Card Premium - Undated
55   Hammond Clock Company Stock Certificate
56   Premium Punch Card 1933
57   Hammond Sealed Rotor Conversion Kit Instructions
61   Sealed Rotor Conversion Kit Warranty Post Card
62   Two Clocks in One Brochure
66   Exact Time Brochure
70   Modern Time Brochure

Gregory Electric Calendar Clock—Tells day, date and exact time. Case is black bakelite in modern design. Day and date change automatically. Height 6½", width at base 5¾"; dial, silver finish, raised numerals...$12.50

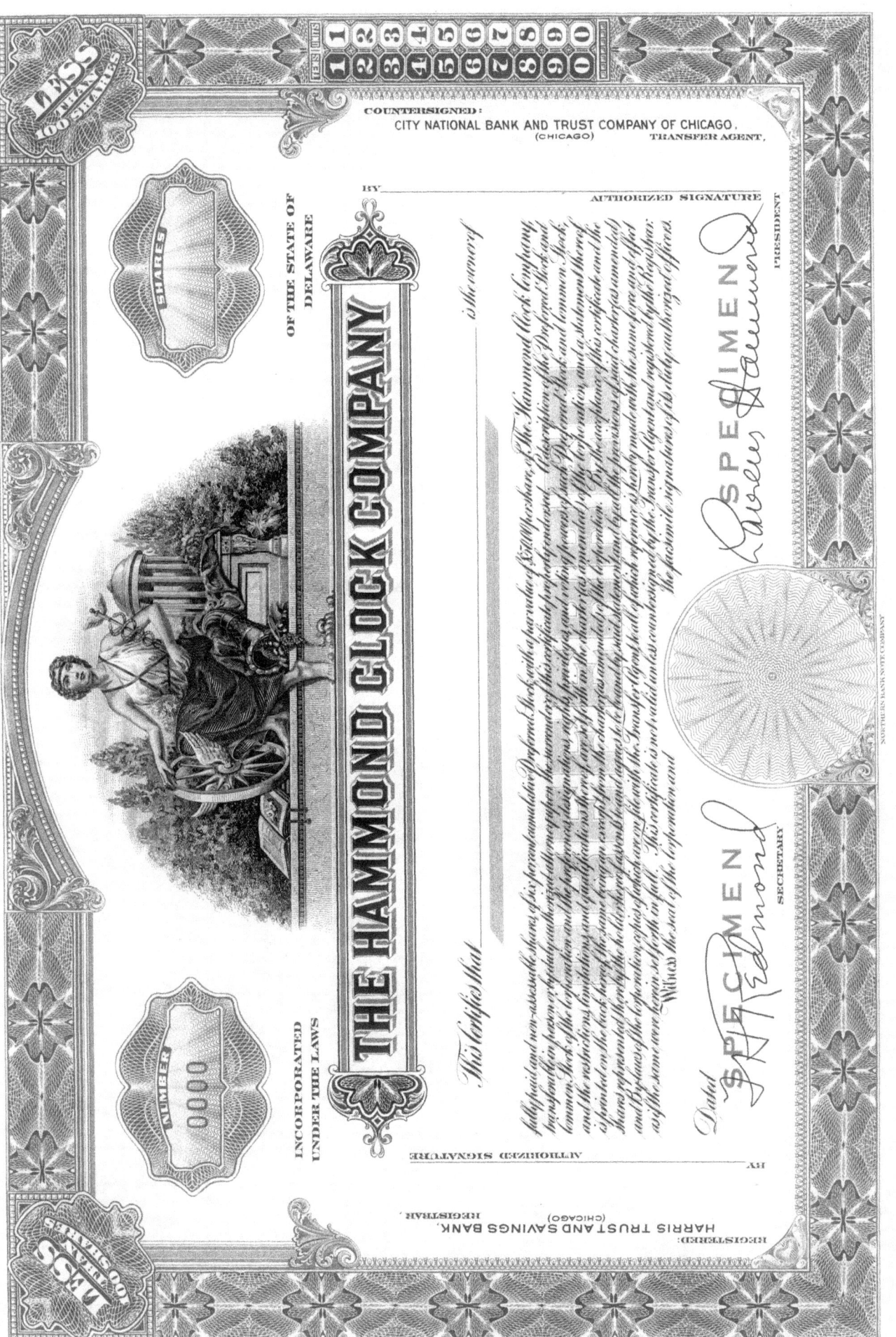

Premium Punch Card 1933

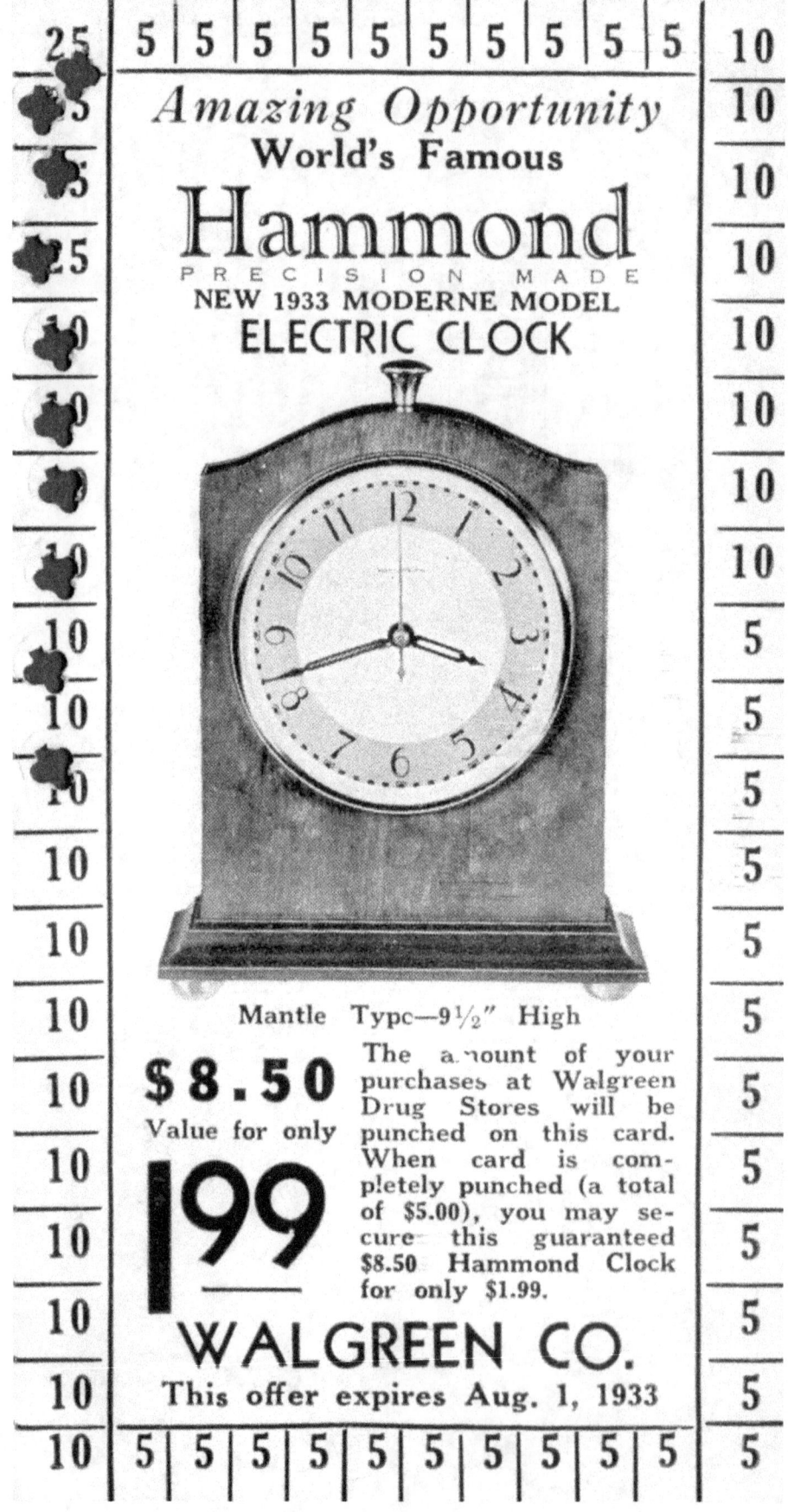

Hammond Electric Clock Kit

Model C

This kit contains:

1 Hammond Electric Clock Movement with special mounting brackets and ten feet of cord.

5 Sets of hands for dials having minute circles in the following approximate sizes:

$3''$, $3\frac{5}{8}''$, $5\frac{3}{8}''$, $5\frac{7}{8}''$, $9\frac{3}{8}''$

2 Rubber Bushings.
2 Hour Hand Bushings.
3 Small Plugs for key holes in dial.
3 Large Plugs for key holes in dial.
1 Two-piece electric plug.
1 Instruction Folder.

This electric clock movement will operate correctly only when connected to a lighting circuit of the voltage and frequency (cycles) indicated on the name plate. Movements are available for use on the following voltages and frequencies:

105–125V. 60 Cycle	105–125V. 25 Cycle
105–125V. 50 Cycle	210–250V. 60 Cycle
105–125V. 30 Cycle	210–250V. 50 Cycle

This movement will keep perfectly correct time when used on the ordinary house lighting circuit in practically all cities of the United States. There are still some communities where the electric light company is not supplying the necessary time service so if there is any doubt, ask the dealer from whom this kit was purchased or, ask your local power company, "do you regulate the frequency so that synchronous clocks may be run on your line?"

Be sure that the voltage and frequency (cycles) of the movement you have is correct for your current supply before installing.

Caution! The Hammond movement should not be used with a steel dial. Care should be taken to see that no large steel parts of the clock case are within 2" of the Hammond movement. Such parts will cause considerable loss of power in the electric motor and are likely to make the clock noisy.

Hammond Electric Clock Conversion Kit Leaflet - 2 of 4
Instructions for Installing

Remove the old mechanism from the clock case, taking care not to damage the dial, hands, and the glass crystal.

The two angle shaped brackets on which the movement is mounted are designed in such a way that the movement may be installed in cases of various sizes. The brackets as supplied can be mounted on the supporting structure in clock cases as large as 17″ wide. In case a smaller space is available, the mounting brackets should be cut off with a hack saw to the desired length. In small cases the mounting brackets may be removed entirely and the movement attached to the supporting structure in the clock case by means of the aluminum plate on which it is mounted. In some instances it will be necessary to trim this small aluminum mounting plate where the space available for the movement is small. With the mounting brackets supplied, installations are possible in a wide variety of clock cases.

The two angle shaped brackets on which the movement is mounted are fastened in a horizontal position. These can be removed from the aluminum mounting plate to which they are bolted and fastened in a vertical position if desired. See Fig. 1.

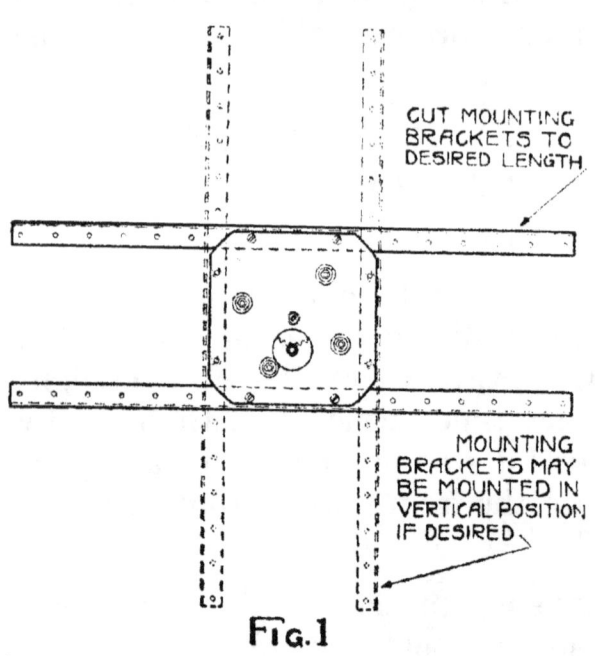

Fig. 1

Note: The face of the aluminum mounting plate should be 7/16″ back of the front face of the dial. Spacing washers can be used between the brackets and the case or between the brackets and the aluminum mounting plate in order that this dimension be maintained accurately. Caution! Before cutting the mounting brackets to size, carefully measure the distance between the mounting holes in the clock case. It is expected that you will use the same dial that was originally used in the clock. If the starting and setting knobs at the rear of the clock will be accessible after the electric movement is installed, it will not be necessary to use the front start shaft and knob shown in figure No. 2, in which case the knob should be pulled off and the shaft cut off with a pair of pliers. In cutting off this shaft it is necessary that it be cut short enough so as not to interfere with the dial. Care should be taken to prevent any twisting while cutting this shaft. If it is desired to start and set the clock from the front, a $^{11}\!/_{32}$" diameter hole should be drilled in the dial to accommodate the front starting shaft. (For location of hole see figure 3.)

Note: The hole in the center of the dial through which the main shaft projects should not be less than $^{5}\!/_{16}$" in diameter.

After the movement and dial have been mounted in the case, the hands should be fastened in place. Select a set of hands of proper size. Remove round brass nut from minute shaft; press on hour hand. Next mount minute hand on minute shaft and replace and tighten nut previously removed. The sweep second hand should then be set on the end of the steel second shaft by tapping with a small hard tool. Caution! Do not strike the second hand bushing with a heavy blow, as it may cause damage to the movement.

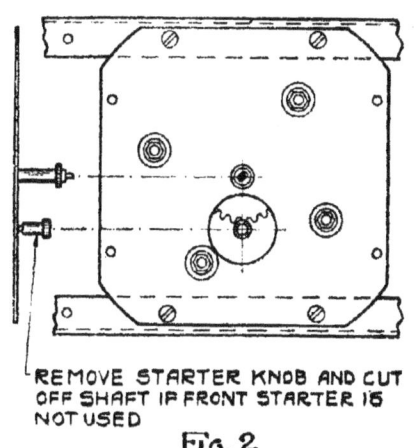

REMOVE STARTER KNOB AND CUT OFF SHAFT IF FRONT STARTER IS NOT USED
Fig. 2

Note: It may be desirable to use the old hour and minute hands. To do so, it may be necessary to change the hole in the minute hand, and to mount one of the small brass bushings in the hour hand. This bushing is furnished with the kit for that purpose. This can be done by riveting the bushing into the hand after the proper size hole has been provided in the hand.

The dial will undoubtedly have two or three key holes in it which are no longer necessary and small nickel plated plugs, washers, and nuts, are provided to fill up these holes in case it is desired to do so. See Fig. 3.

The clock should be fitted with rubber or felt feet. This will prevent scratching of the mantel or furniture and will absorb some of the 60 cycle vibration that is always present in an electric clock.

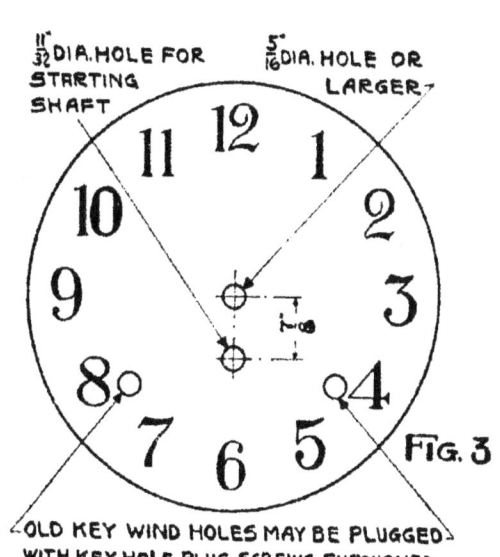

OLD KEY WIND HOLES MAY BE PLUGGED WITH KEY HOLE PLUG SCREWS FURNISHED
Fig. 3

Operating Instructions

1. Plug into socket which cannot be turned off.

2. Set clock to correct time by means of large setting knob on back of clock or by moving hands on front.

If the clock is set from the back the second hand may be set by turning the starter.

3. To start clock turn small starting knob on the back of the clock, pressing in gently at the same time; turn, then let go. Turn starter to left. If started in the wrong direction the clock will run backwards.

If the front starter is used, press the tip of your forefinger against the button and spin to the left; then let go.

Temperature Note: If the clock is cold when first connected to a line it may stop occasionally during the first few hours of operation due to congealed oil in the motor which runs in oil. After being connected to current supply for several hours it will be thoroughly warmed up and will operate normally thereafter.

Be sure you have correct time when setting as any error will continue as a permanent error until you reset the clock. (Use a radio signal when possible, to get correct time).

REMEMBER, if the current is turned off even momentarily the clock will stop and will require re-starting and re-setting. AS LONG AS IT IS RUNNING IT WILL INDICATE CORRECT TIME.

The Hammond Synchronous Electric Clock is manufactured in the U. S. A. under patent Nos. 1,719,805, RE17,779 and applications.

The Hammond Clock Company

2915 N. WESTERN AVENUE
CHICAGO, ILL.

Form KI—Printed in U. S. A.

GUARANTEE

This electric clock movement is fully guaranteed by The Hammond Clock Company, Chicago, subject to the following conditions:

Any part or parts proving defective within one year from date of purchase will be replaced or repaired without expense to the customer other than transportation charges.

This guarantee does not apply to any movement used on a current supply different from that indicated on the name plate of the clock. Any evidence of tampering with the movement will be sufficient cause to invalidate the guarantee. To make this guarantee effective and to establish the duration of the guarantee period, a record of your purchase must be filed with The Hammond Clock Company. To do this, fill out the other part of this card and mail it at once. If the card is not mailed to The Hammond Clock Company, the factory record for the guarantee period will govern the expiration date of the free replacement period.

SERVICE

If you have reason to think that your clock is not operating properly, return it to the local dealer who can repair it for you or write direct to the Service Department of The Hammond Clock Company, Chicago, Illinois, for instructions and advice. Describe the difficulty as fully as possible and DO NOT return the clock before writing, as the necessity for doing so can usually be eliminated.

NOTICE

This clock movement is equipped with a Hammond Type "C" synchronous electric clock motor which is detachable. The motor unit is sealed in a container and runs in oil. This type of construction assures a long period of satisfactory service and eliminates the need for attention or oiling.

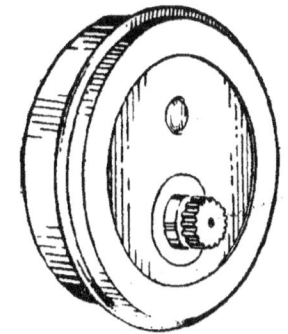

Type C Motor

If the motor should ever wear out or require service, your clock can be given an entirely new span of life by merely replacing the motor. Your local dealer can install a new motor for a small charge or you may obtain full instructions from The Hammond Clock Company.

YOUR RECORD

Guarantee Card mailed........................
　　　　　　　　　　　　　　　(date)

　　　　　　Serial No.....................

Form KG

The Stewardess — For kitchen, office or den. Case—5½" high, 6¾" wide. Colors: ivory, green, red, black or white, with chrome-plated fluted side bands and bezel. Dial 5⅛" by 4⅝". Legible black figures and hands on white background.

The Parkway — For kitchen or bath. Furnished in ivory, green or red. Case 6⅞" diameter. Dial 4¾" with legible black figures and hands.

The Prudence — Enamel finished metal face with bright metal trim, 6¼" square. White finished metal dial, 4¼". Colors: ivory, red, white, black, green.

THE Regent — Lustrous genuine white onyx easel type case 5⅛" square. Hand-spun gold-plated 4⅜" dial with white hour markings, gold-plated hands and revolving second disc. Alarm.

THE Courtier — Easel style wood case, 5⅝" high, 4⅛" wide. Highly figured butt walnut face. 3½" silver-plated dial. Alarm.

THE Edgemont — Easel type bright chrome finish case, 4⅝" high, 5¼" wide. Silver-plated satin finish dial, 4" by 4½" with black numerals and hands. Alarm.

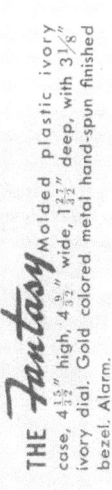

THE Fantasy — Molded plastic ivory case, 4 15/32" high, 4 9/32" wide, 1 27/32" deep, with 3⅜" ivory dial. Gold colored metal hand-spun finished bezel. Alarm.

THE Grenadier — Sparkling chrome-plated easel type case, 5½" high, 4¾" wide. Dial—silver-plated two-tone 4¼" with black numerals and hands. Black stripe across base. Alarm.

THE Cathay — Ivory finish plastic case 4 1/16" high, 3⅞" wide, 1⅝" deep. Dial 3⅛". Black numerals and hands. Gold finished bezel and feet. Alarm.

Hammond Ephemera

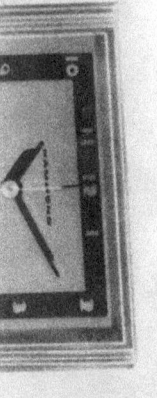
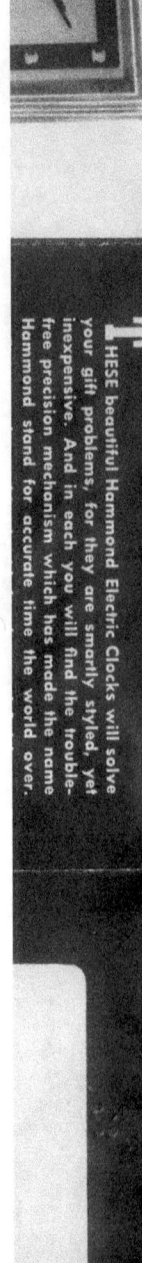

THESE beautiful Hammond Electric Clocks will solve your gift problems, for they are smartly styled, yet inexpensive. And in each you will find the trouble-free precision mechanism which has made the name Hammond stand for accurate time the world over.

Exclusive HAMMOND FEATURES

You tell time easily in the dark with the Luna and Modern Firefly alarm clocks. A hidden bulb, tiny and long-lived, lights the translucent dial, without glare. Notice also the ingenious combination of time, alarm and automatic calendar, showing both day and date, in the Tripoli. These unusual features make these the last word in distinctive gift clocks.

THE *Pilot*

Serves beautifully on the mantel as well as on radio, table, bookcase or desk. Solid mahogany case with walnut burl finish face—7 3/16" square, 3 3/8" deep. Etched white silver-plated dial with gold color satin finish rings, diameter 5". Black metal hands, gold finished second hand. Alarm.

The *Dayton*

A beautiful mantel clock of striking modern design. Has the popular Hammond automatic calendar, showing day and date. Selected striped mahogany veneer case—5 5/8" high, 7 13/16" wide, 3 3/32" deep. Silver-plated gold color numeral frame, satin finish—5 1/8" by 3 3/4". Face: 4-piece matched sapeli. Solid Mahogany base.

The *Tripoli*

An exceptional gift clock—right at home on desk, library table, bookshelf or radio. Combines time, alarm and automatic calendar, showing day and date. Striped mahogany veneer case of fine burl finish—5 1/4" high, 6 1/2" wide, 3" deep. Silver-plated, two-tone dial—3 1/2".

The *Luna*

A very distinctive bedroom clock, with the popular Hammond Soft Glow dial. Solid mahogany case—5 3/8" high, 5 3/16" wide, 2 9/16" deep. Amboyne burl finish face. Gold color metal polish finished bezel. Translucent plastic dial, 3 1/8", illuminated without glare by tiny bulb. Alarm.

The *Modern Firefly*

An illuminated "Soft Glow" dial alarm clock. Molded plastic case 5 1/4" high, 4 1/2" wide, 2 1/16" deep. Furnished in ivory with gold finished trim and feet or black with chrome plate trim and feet. The illuminated 3" translucent "Soft Glow" dial tells time in the dark without glare.

Hammond Electric Clocks

THESE beautiful Hammond Electric Clocks will solve your gift problems, for they are smartly styled, yet inexpensive. And in each you will find the trouble-free precision mechanism which has made the name Hammond stand for accurate time the world over.

Fine woods combined with lovely metal finishes—lasting beauty of design—dependability—long life—all mean HAMMOND, the most prized gift of all.

HAMMOND Electric Clocks are accurate. When properly set, they "can never be running and be wrong."

HAMMOND Clocks have slow speed motors for quiet operation and long life.

HAMMOND Clocks are properly styled, beautifully designed.

HAMMOND Clocks are approved by the Underwriters' Laboratories.

HAMMOND Clocks are guaranteed for one full year against mechanical and electrical defects.

Only HAMMOND builds an alarm with the "Soft Glow dial which tells time in the dark."

Only HAMMOND offers "two clocks in one"—an alarm at no extra cost on most models.

Only HAMMOND provides a clock combining time, alarm and automatic calendar.

There are many millions of HAMMOND Clocks giving continuous care-free service to their satisfied owners.

HAMMOND INSTRUMENT COMPANY
2915 N. WESTERN AVE.   CHICAGO, ILL.

Makers of the Hammond Organ, Novachord, Solovox

CHICAGO, ILLINOIS

Litho in United States of America

C-118-5-41

Hammond *Exclusive* FEATURES

THE *Riviera* A superbly graceful design for table and desk. Satin finish, gold-plated case, 4 13/32" high, 6 5/8" wide. Metal feet. Gold color satin finish dial, 3 13/32" by 5 5/8"; black numeral frame. Black metal hands; gold colored second hand with black tip. Alarm.

THE *Chancellor* Rich walnut case faced with center matched stump walnut—light stripe inlay on front and sides. Case—8 5/8" high, 7 5/8" wide, 3 1/4" deep. 5" dial with hand-spun silver-plated ring on etched white silver-plated field.

Hammond Clocks Will Not Work on Direct Current (D. C.)

The Hammond All-Electric Clock is of the synchronous type made to take advantage of the free time service now being supplied by most power companies. It is not merely electrically wound but registers the pulsations of the alternating current. Therefore, it will not work on direct current. All models are designed to operate on 80-135 volts and give exact time where time service is supplied. Fluctuations in line voltage do not affect the operation of these clocks since they are regulated entirely by the frequency.

All models are furnished for operation on standard frequencies. Unless specified, sixty cycle will be furnished.

The Hammond Synchronous Electric Clock is manufactured in the U. S. A. under Hammond patent 1,719,805 and applications.

The HAMMOND CLOCK Company

2915 N. WESTERN AVENUE
CHICAGO, ILL.

DISTRIBUTED BY

PRINTED IN U. S. A.
FORM C-7

EXACT TIME
...for the Home
...by Electricity

HAMMOND ELECTRIC CLOCKS

Ten Beautiful Models
Priced from $9.75 to $32.50 ▲ No Reason

How You Can Get Exact Time from » » » »
« « « « « the Light Socket in Your Home

YOU need no longer wind the family clocks... or even regulate them... for the modern way of telling time is by electricity. Just as electricity efficiently performs other household duties, so it serves to bring exact time.

You will marvel at the constant accuracy maintained by the Hammond All-Electric Clock... an accuracy that clockmakers have long sought to obtain is now made possible by electricity.

This new way is convenient. You never wind a Hammomd Clock for it has no springs. It is not necessary to regulate because the same electricity that runs the clock also regulates it. This is accomplished as follows: The power company supplies alternating current, which kind of current contains regular and rapid pulsations. These pulsations are kept at a constant rate by means of master clock equipment at the power station so that your Hammond Clock, made to register them, will receive an exact number of pulsations per second. Most power companies maintain this free time-service for their consumers. It is known as regulating the frequency.

Hammond All-Electric Clocks are made in various models and colors as shown on the inside of this folder. You will notice there are styles for every room in the home, and the prices are so low that you will want several of these modern timepieces that never require attention.

The New Ravenswood with Electric Alarm with all the features of Hammond Clocks is the ideal boudoir timepiece. A flip of the switch at bed time is the only attention required. Has buzzer alarm. Other description same as the Ravenswood. Priced at $12.50

▲ One for Every Purpose
Reason Now to be Without this New Convenience

CT TIME KEEPERS

The Kitchen Series — The housewife knows the importance of correct time in the kitchen. Available in white, blue, green, yellow or brown; metal case 8½" wide, dial 5½". Convex crystal sealed to protect dial. Priced at . . $9.75

. . without winding est gift of electricity. maintained by the always refer to it be right . . . bound egulated.

mechanical escape- , a small synchro- registers the time- to it by the elec- e light socket. It is e by merely insert- to any convenience- the hands in the

usual manner and starting. Thereafter, the same electricity that drives the clock also regulates it so that it keeps exact time. The current consumed is two watts, a negligible amount that costs less than ten cents per month.

Every model is well designed to suit the purpose for which it is intended. A large sweep second hand is included so that the time can be set to the exact second and a flasher disc shows at a glance that the clock is running. Every home, store and office needs at least one clock that is always right.

The Gothic Model—A beautiful mantel clock with walnut case and spun silver dial. Like all other Hammond models, tells exact time without regulating. Height 12", base 4¾" x 9¾", 5½" dial. Priced at . . . $29.50

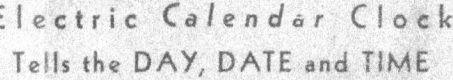

Electric Calendar Clock
Tells the DAY, DATE and TIME

The Gregory—Here is something entirely new in Electric Clocks. Tells the day, date and exact time. Case is black bakelite 6½ x 5¾ dial, silver finished 3¼ x 4¾. Day and date change automatically at midnight. A beautiful and modern electric clock that performs an additional duty. Priced at $12.50

The Cambridge—This is the deluxe tambour model. Note the hand carved solid walnut bezel ring instead of the metal bezel. This clock has walnut case 20" wide and 9" high; spun silver dial 5½" in diameter; separable cord and plug. An elegant mantel clock at $32.50

The Hammond Electric Clock

is of the synchronous electric type. It is regulated by the pulsations (frequency) of the alternating current. Most power companies regulate the pulsations of the current so that synchronous electric clocks tell off exact time.

All models are designed to operate on 80 to 135 volts alternating current. Sixty cycle current is the kind most commonly used and unless specified, sixty cycle models will be supplied. Models for other standard frequencies can be furnished.

The current consumed is two watts and costs less than ten cents a month.

The Hammond Synchronous Electric Clock is manufactured in the U.S.A. under patent Nos. 1,719,805, RE 17,779 and applications.

The Hammond Clock Company

2915 N. WESTERN AVE.
CHICAGO, ILL.

Distributed by

Form C-10   Printed in the U.S.A.

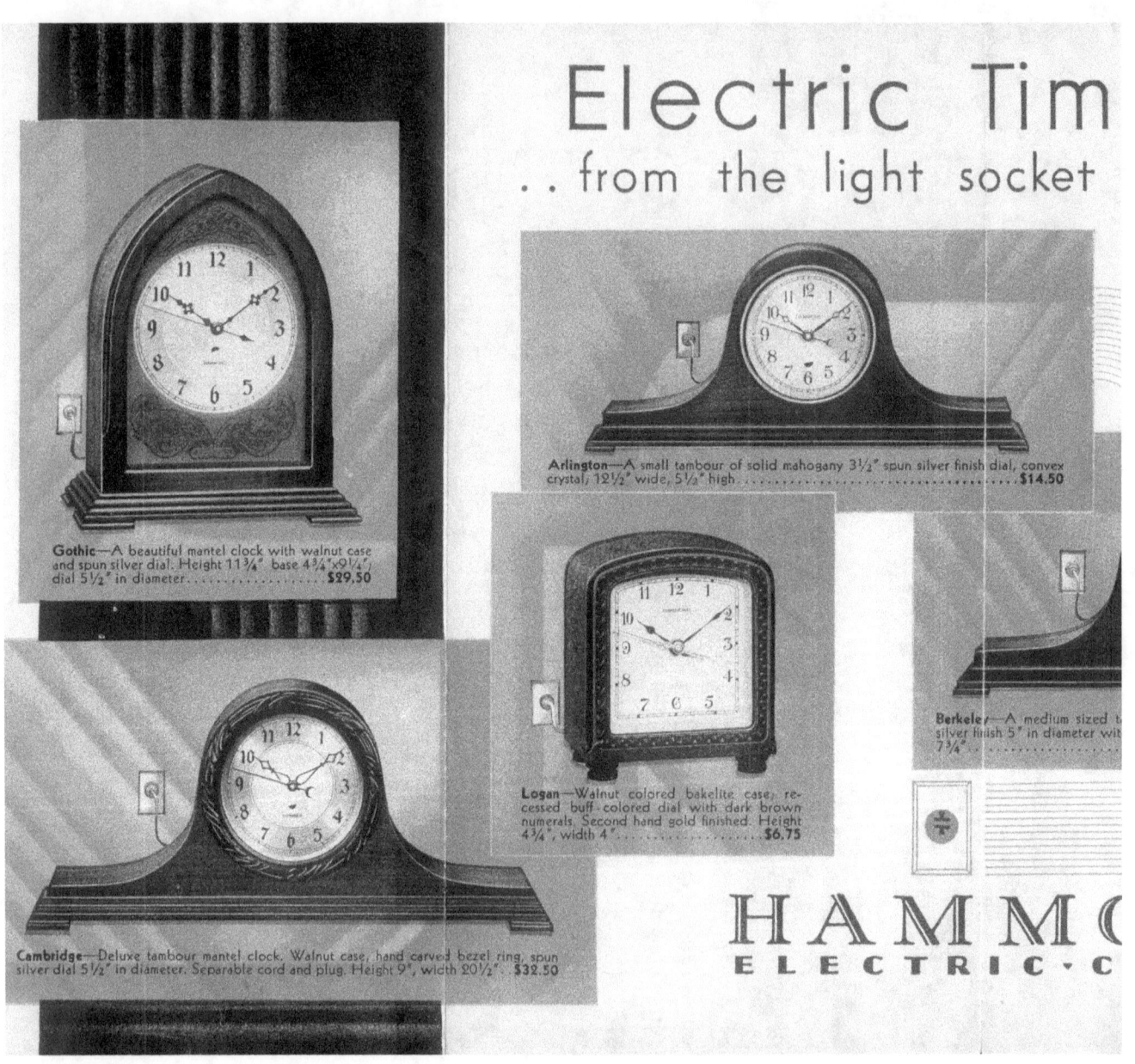

Hammond Patent Drawings

76	July 6, 1920	Utility Patent	Clock
77	July 2, 1929	Utility Patent	Alternating Current Clock
78	March 24, 1931	Utility Patent	Alternating Current Clock
79	December 25, 1934	Utility Patent	Calendar Clock
80	May 21, 1935	Utility Patent	Electric Timepiece
81	May 28, 1935	Utility Patent	Electric Clock Motor
82	September 3, 1935	Utility Patent	Electric Clock
83	January 14, 1936	Utility Patent	Electric Alarm Clock
84	May 26, 1936	Utility Patent	Calendar Clock
85	January 12, 1937	Utility Patent	Electric Clock
86	December 31, 1940	Utility Patent	Illuminated Dial Clock
87	April 28, 1942	Utility Patent	Clock
88	August 26, 1930	Utility Patent	Synchronous Motor
89	May 26, 1931	Design Patent	Clock Case
90	September 1, 1931	Design Patent	Clock Dial
91	September 1, 1931	Design Patent	Clock Case
92	September 8, 1931	Design Patent	Clock Case
93	September 8, 1931	Design Patent	Clock Case
94	December 8, 1931	Design Patent	Combined Dial and Hands
95	December 8, 1931	Design Patent	Combined Dial and Hands
96	March 15, 1932	Design Patent	Clock Case
97	November 29, 1932	Utility Patent	Card Table

L. HAMMOND.
CLOCK.
APPLICATION FILED JULY 14, 1919.

RE15,299
1,345,766.

Patented July 6, 1920.

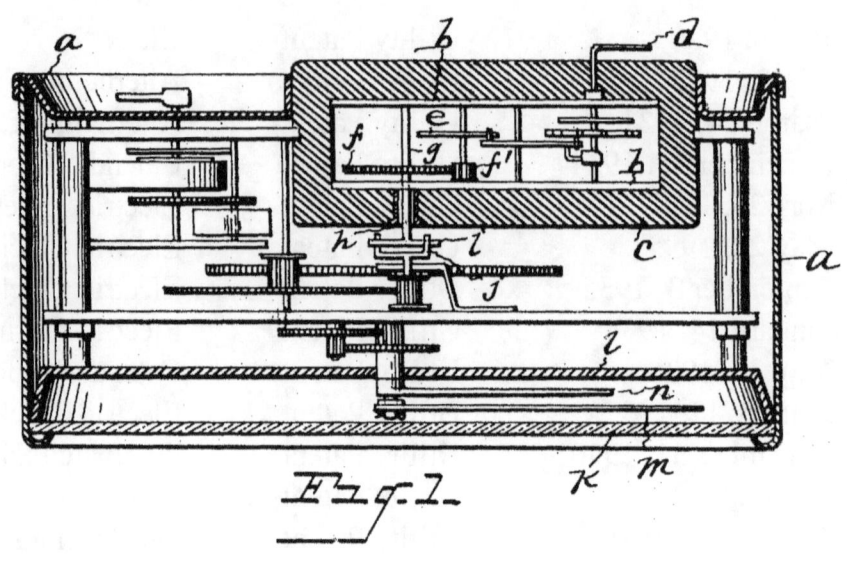

Fig. 1.

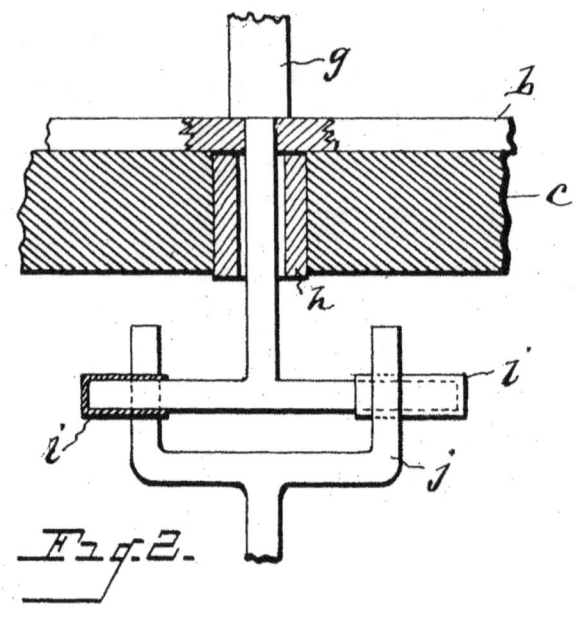

Fig. 2.

Inventor
LAURENS HAMMOND.
By Ralzemond A. Parker
Attorney

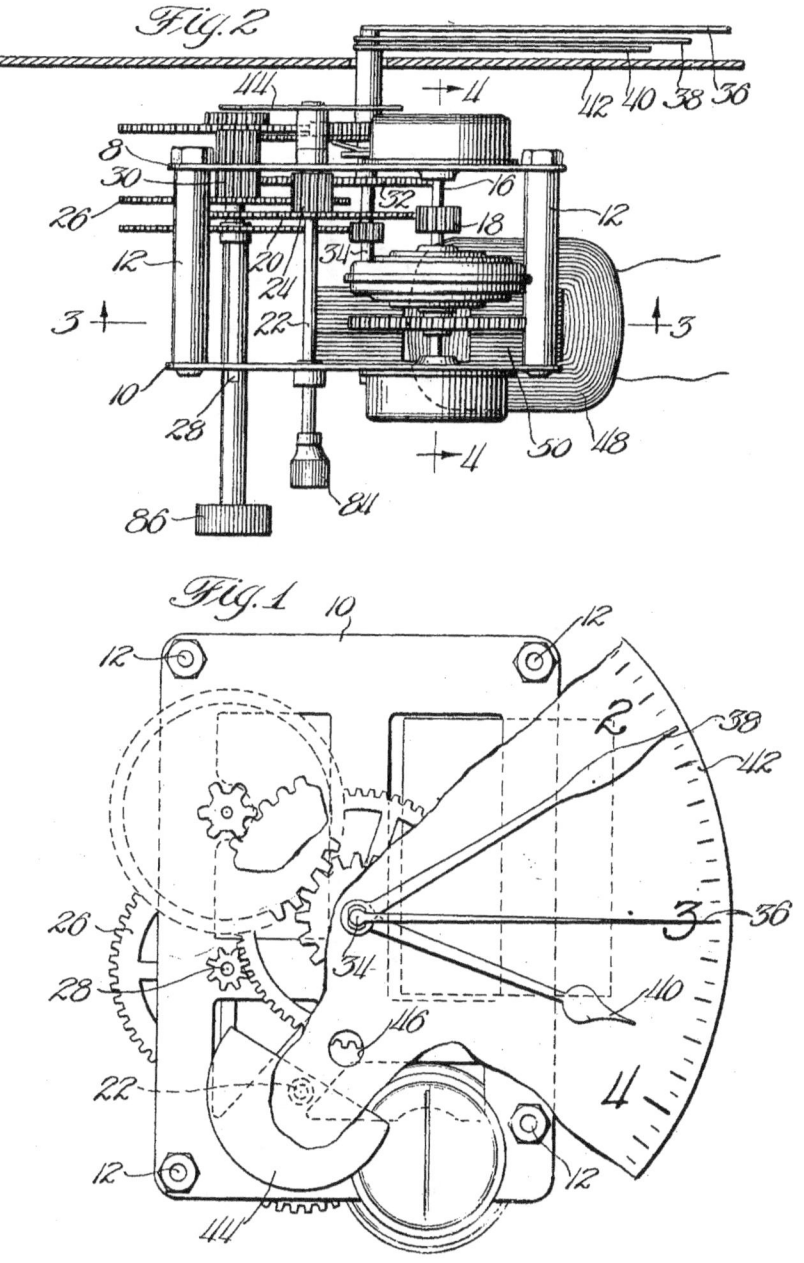

March 24, 1931.   L. HAMMOND   1,797,912
ALTERNATING CURRENT CLOCK
Filed June 18, 1929   3 Sheets—Sheet

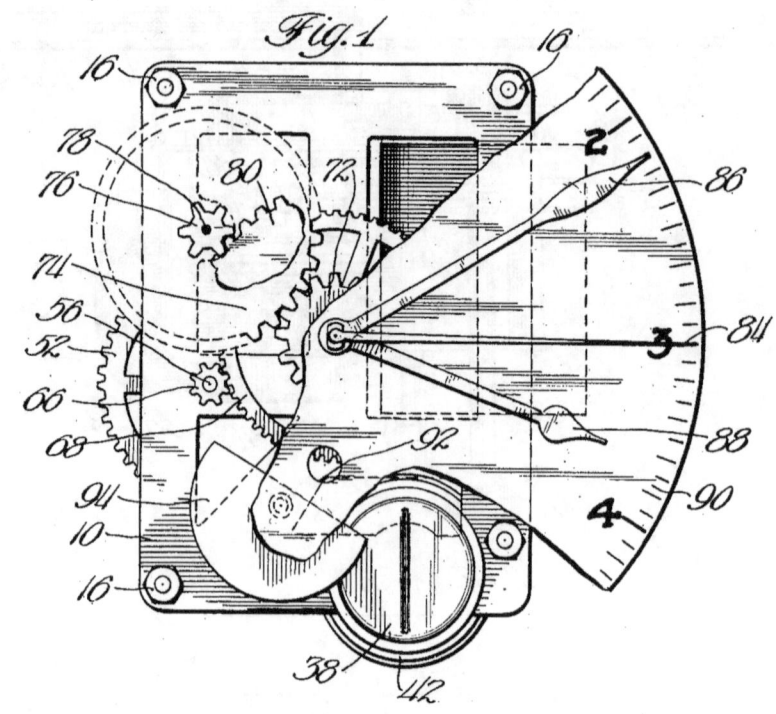

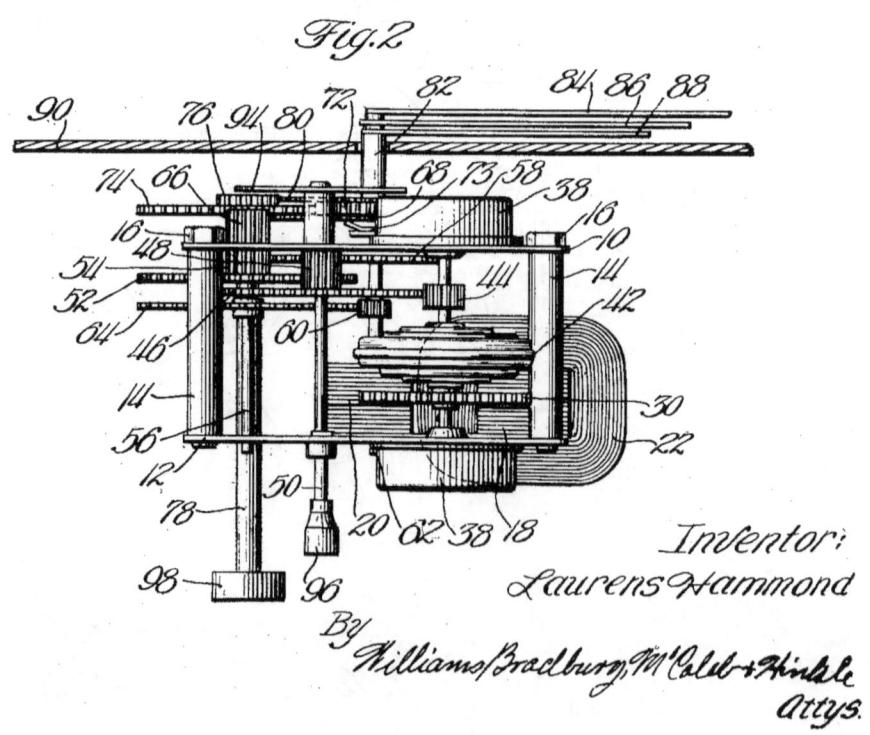

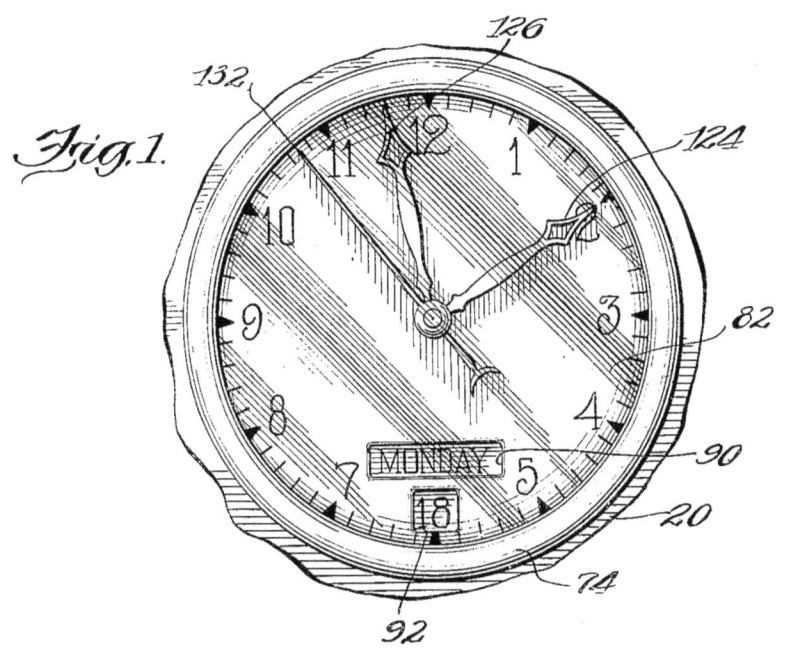
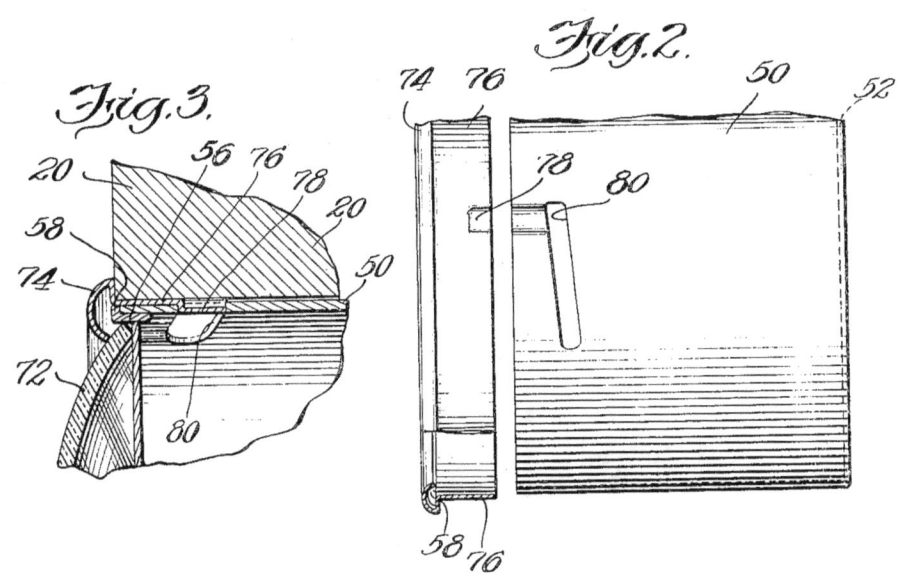

May 21, 1935. L. TISSEYRE ET AL 2,002,421
ELECTRIC TIMEPIECE
Filed May 20, 1929

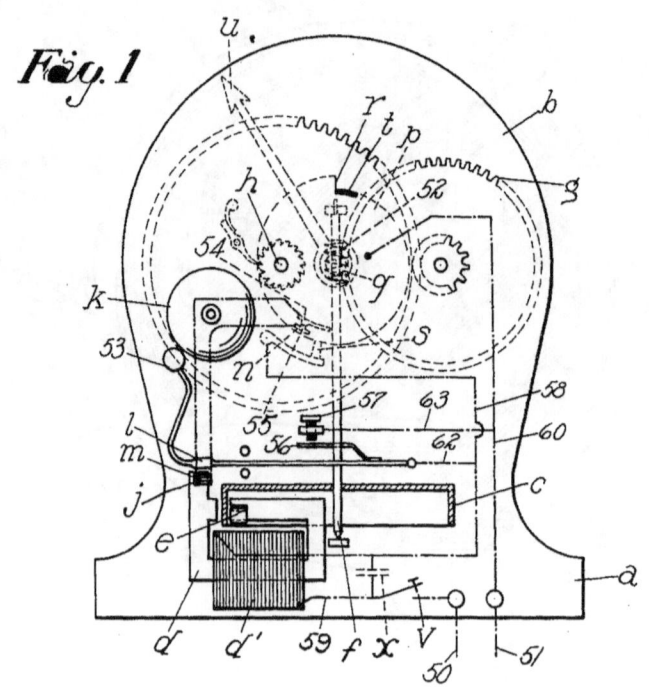

Fig. 1

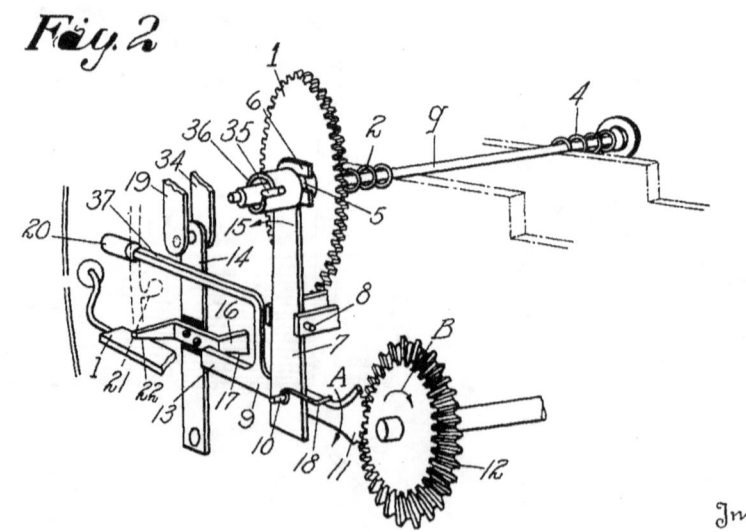

Fig. 2

Inventor
Louis Tisseyre
Ionel Cotnareanu
By W. Clay Lindsey
Attorney

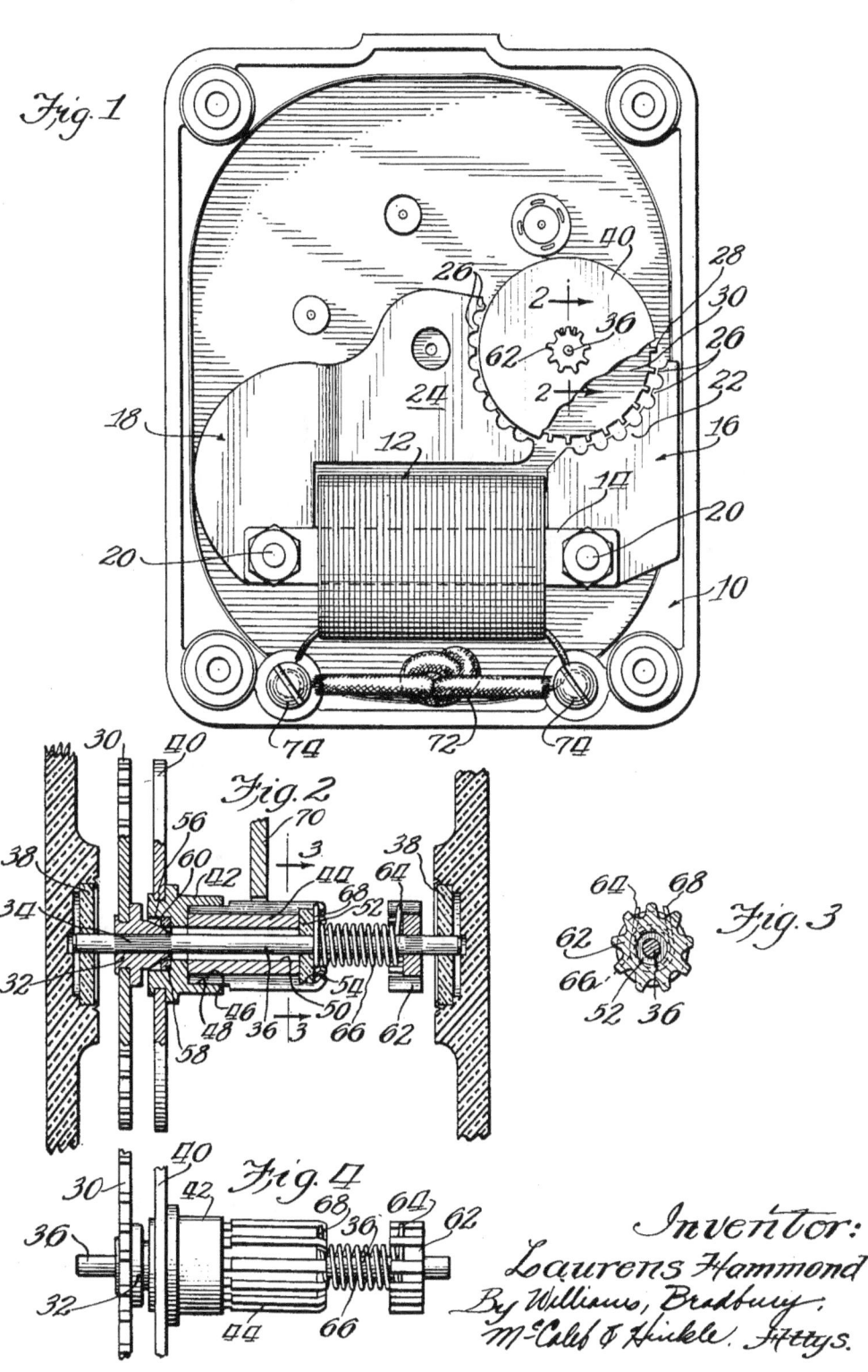

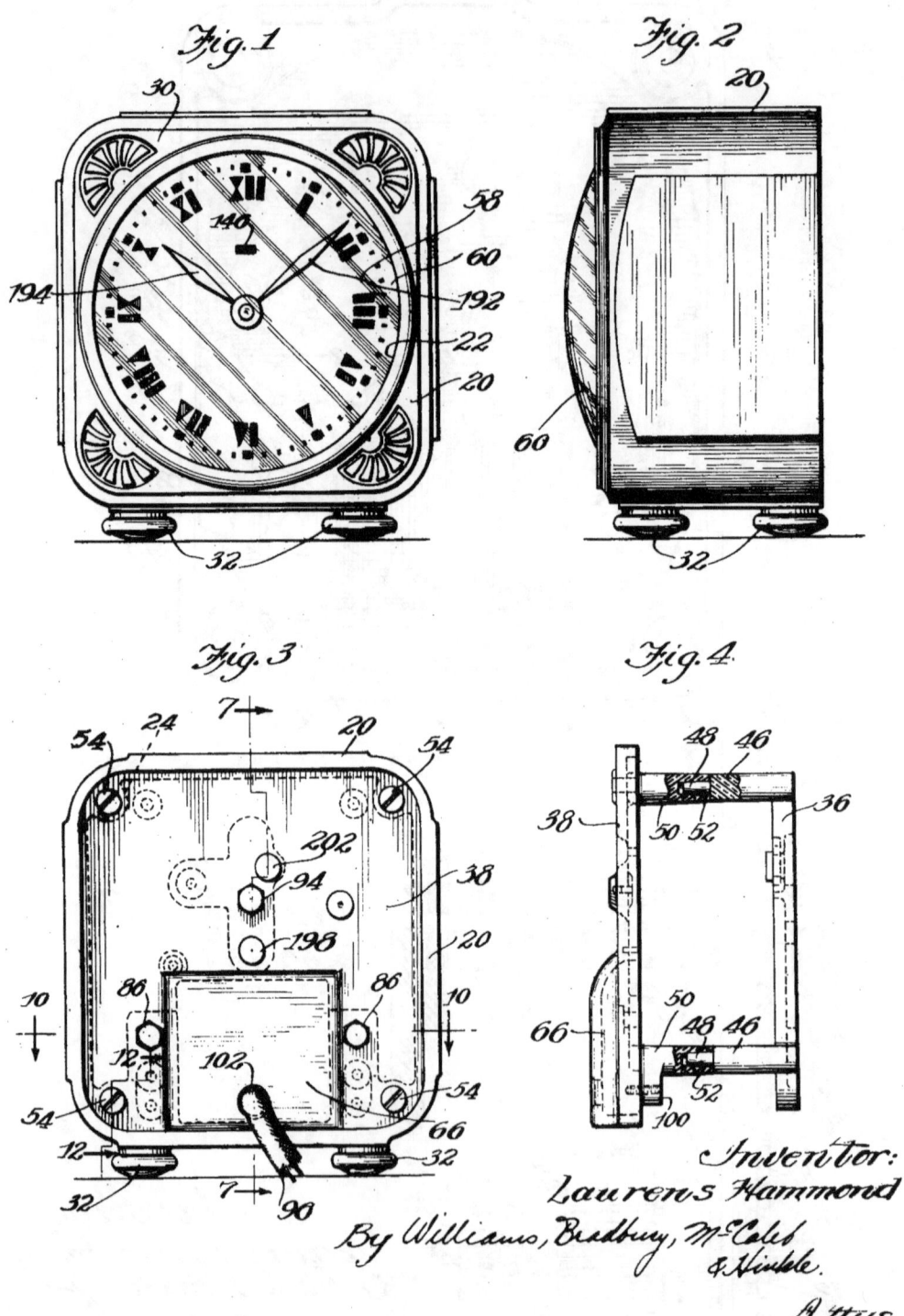

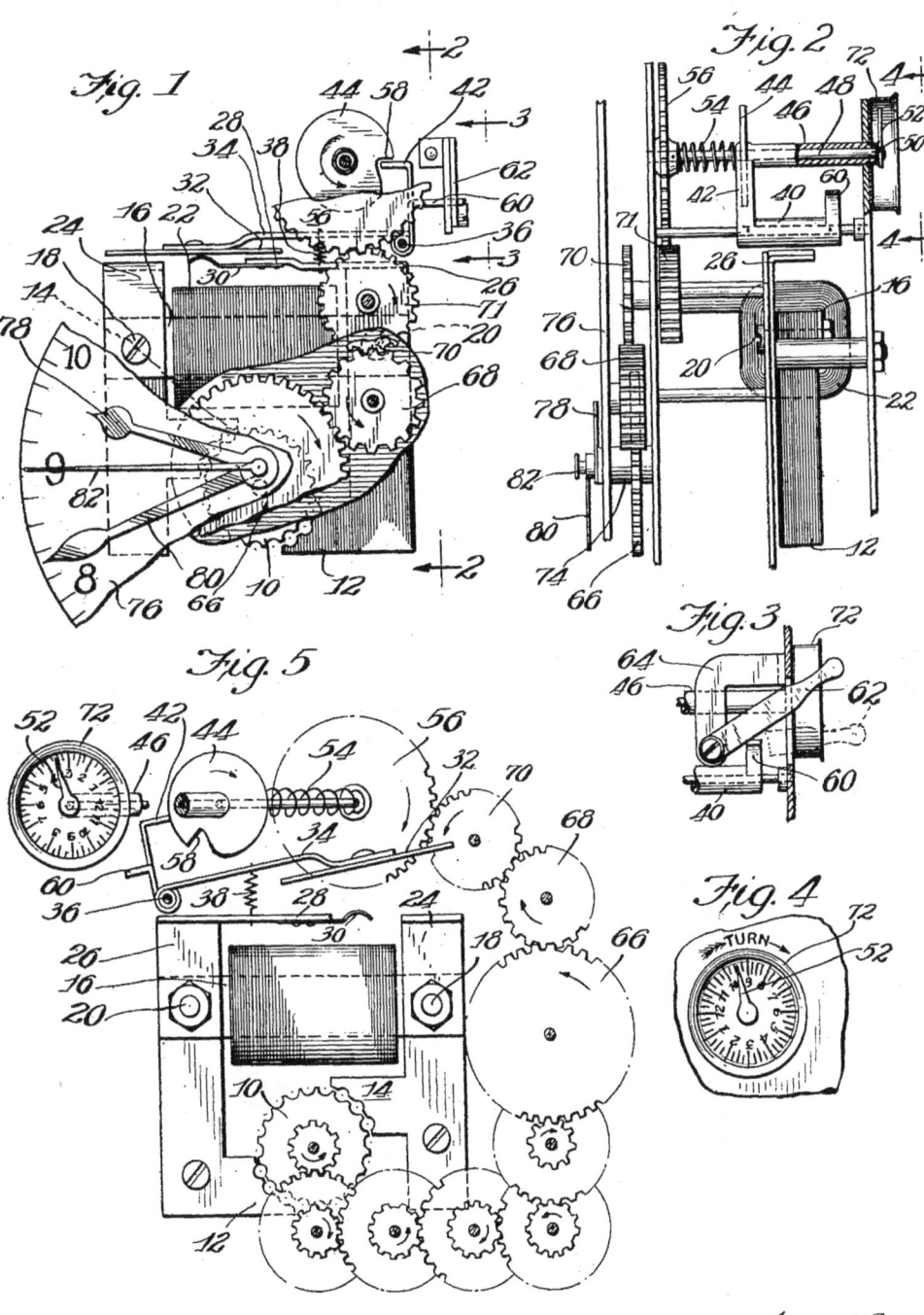

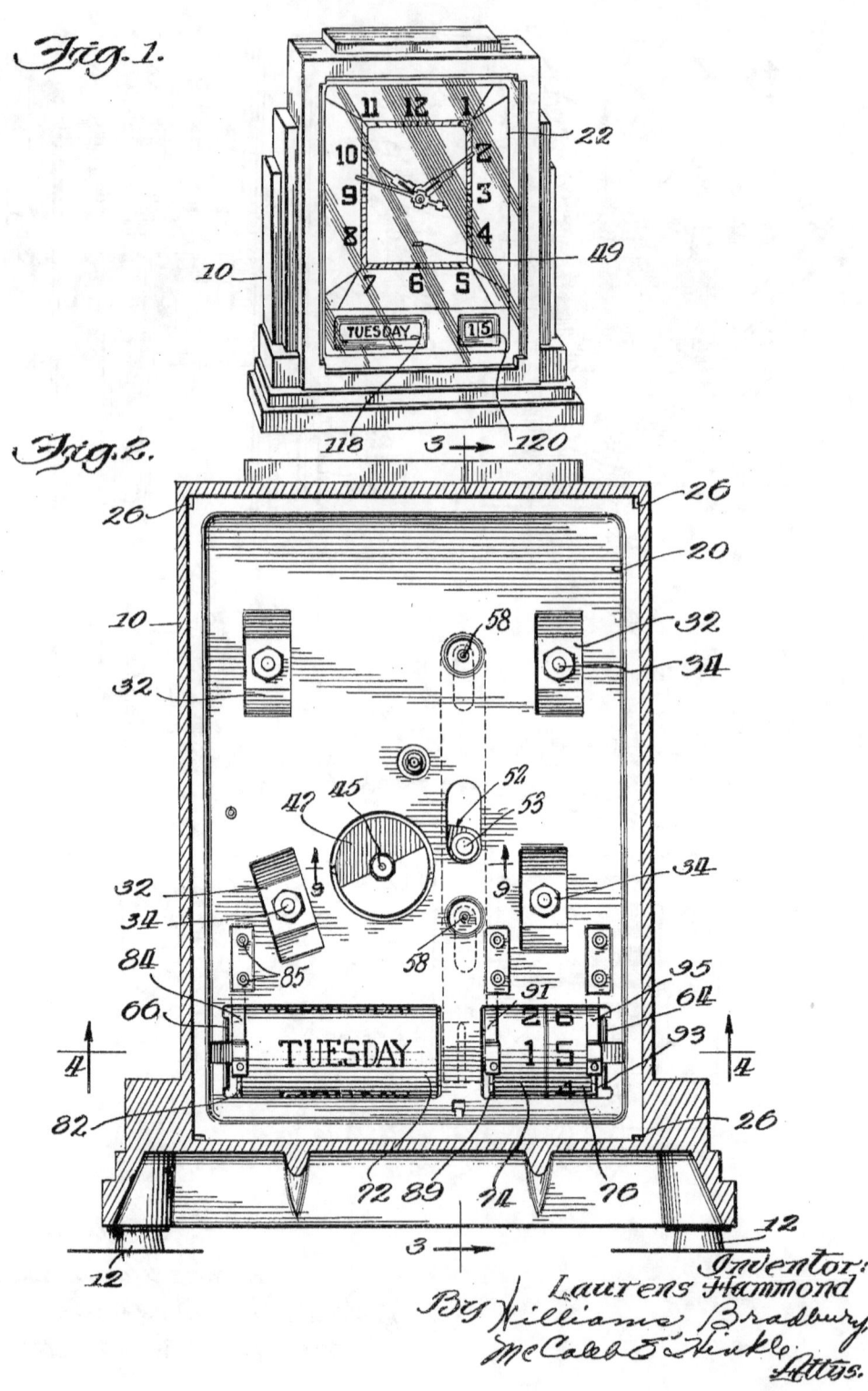

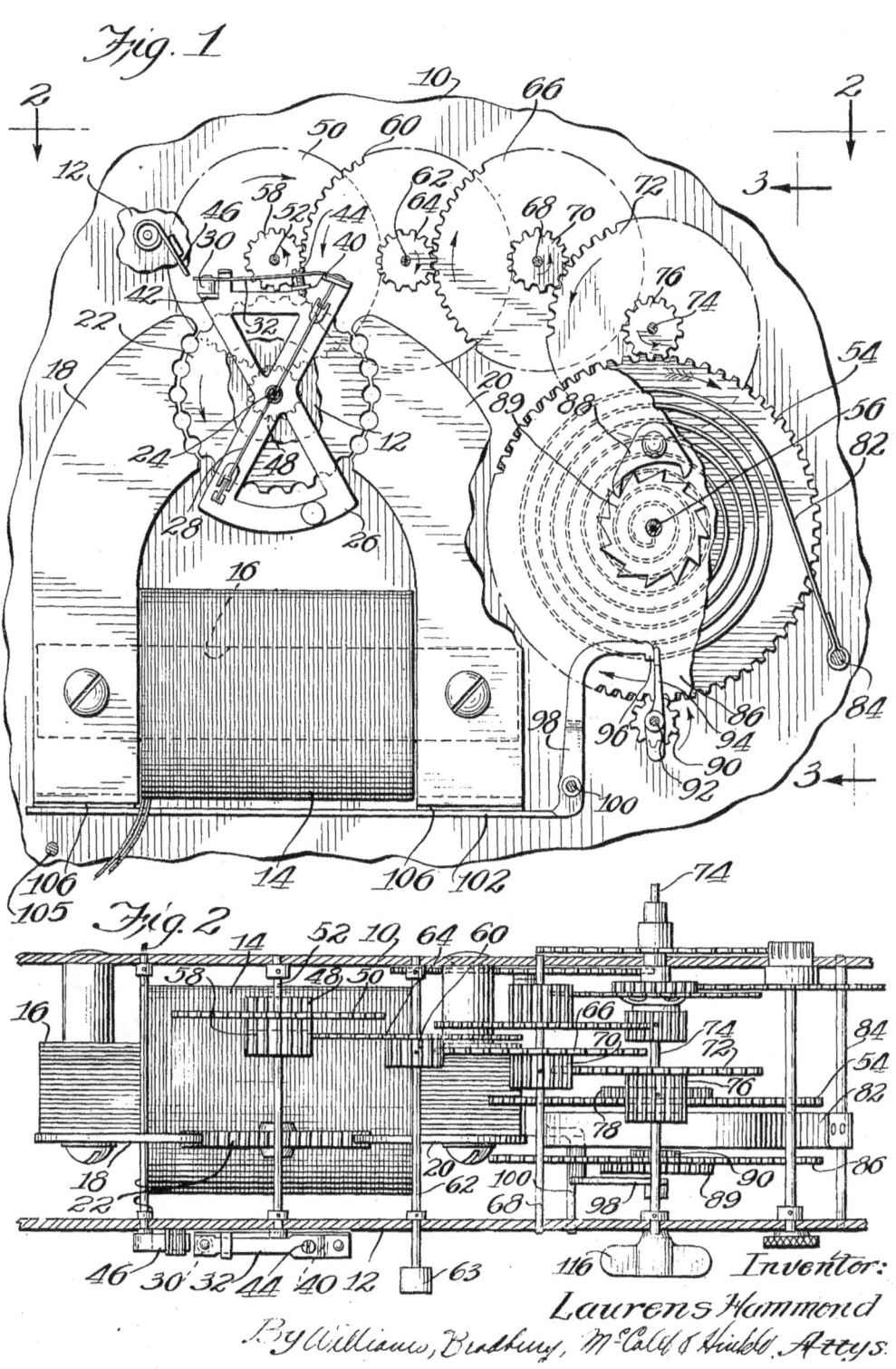

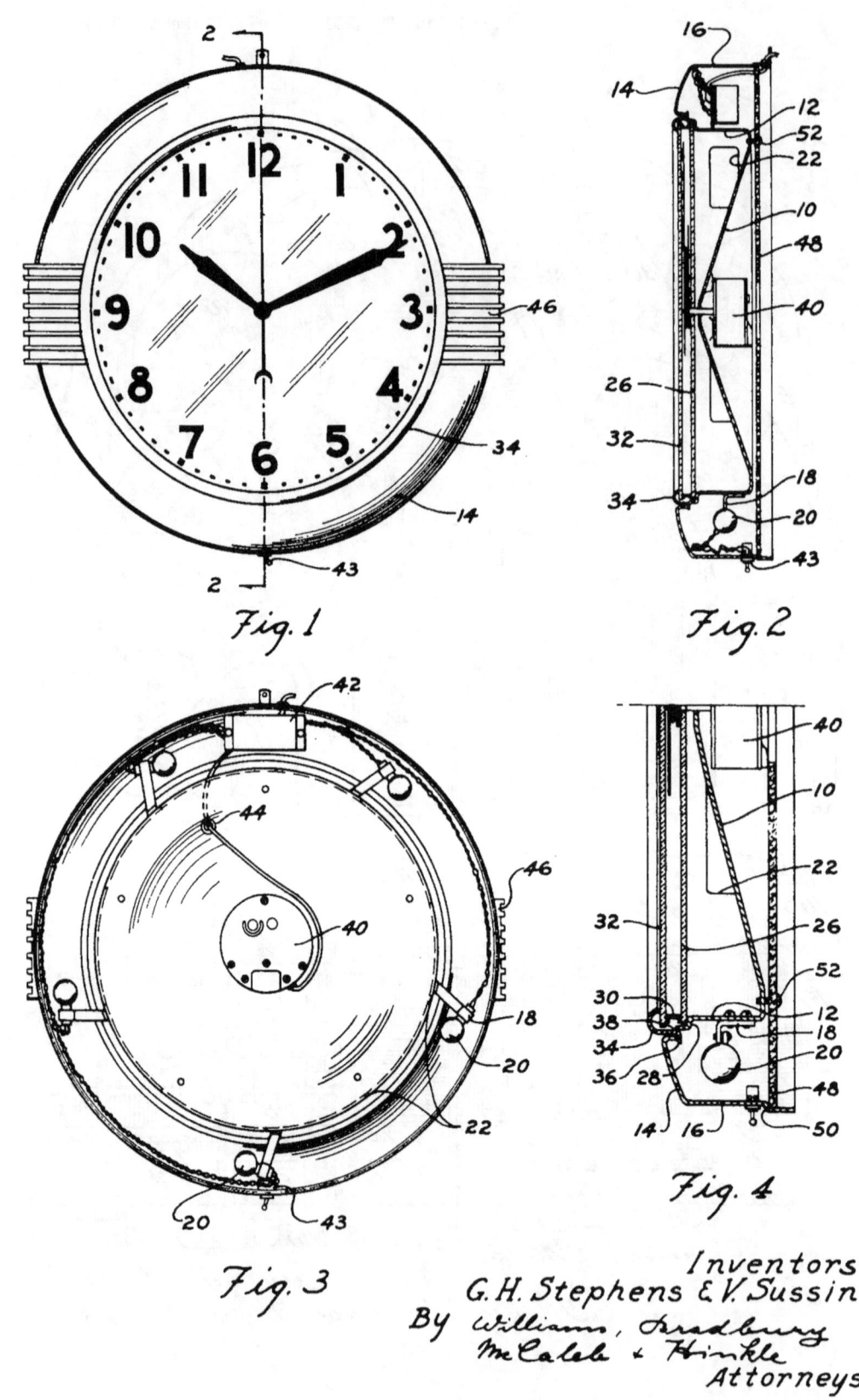

April 28, 1942.　　　L. HAMMOND　　　2,281,494
CLOCK
Filed Feb. 13, 1931　　　5 Sheets-Sheet 1

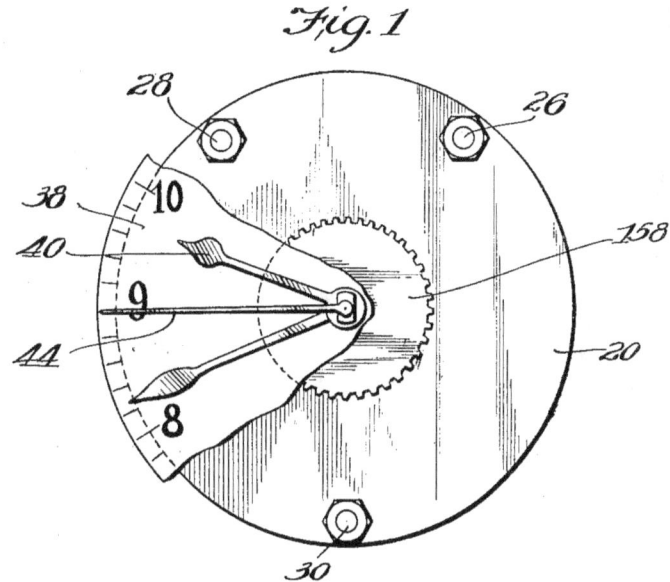

Fig. 1

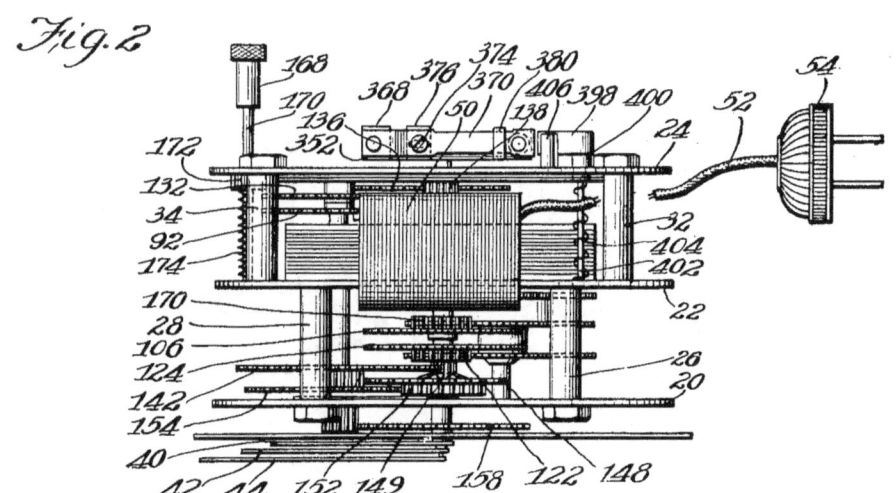

Fig. 2

Inventor:
Laurens Hammond
By Williams, Bradbury, McCaleb
& Hinkle. Attys.

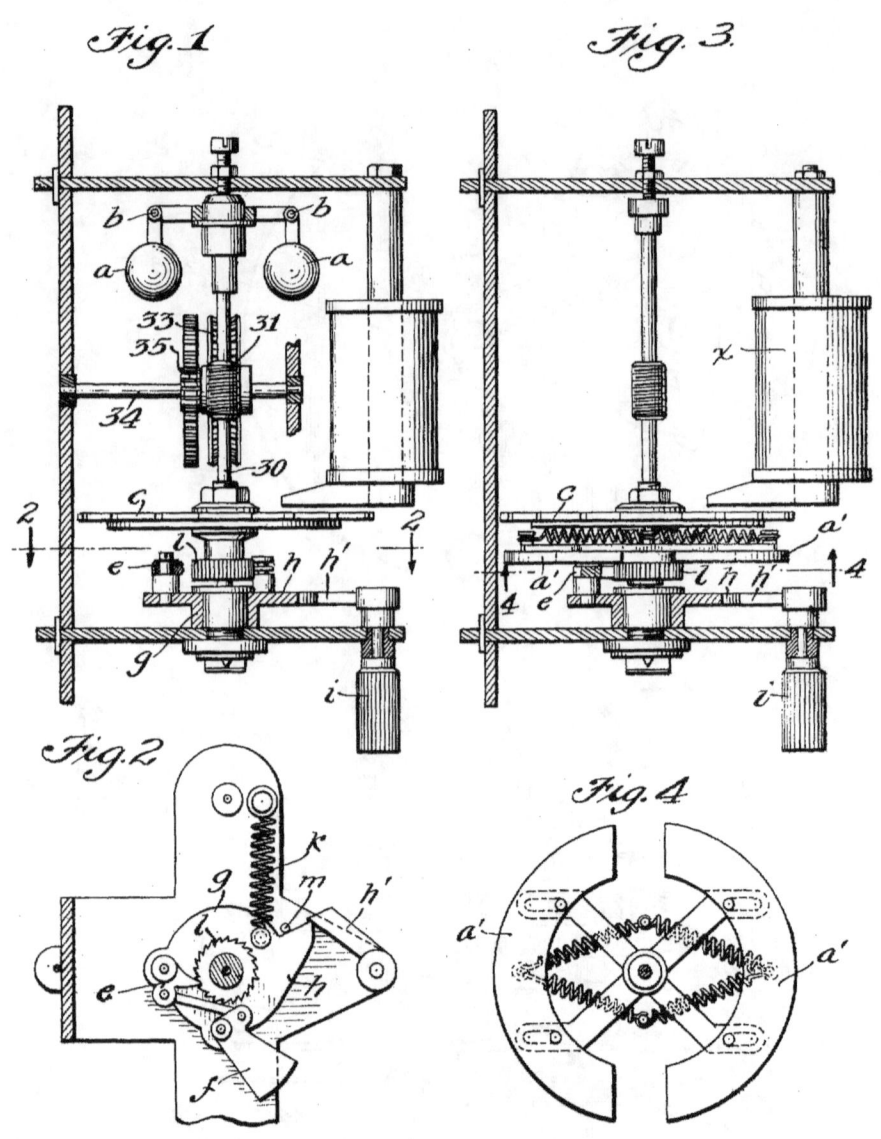

May 26, 1931. G. H. STEPHENS Des. 84,263
CLOCK CASE
Filed March 14, 1931

Sept. 1, 1931.   G. H. STEPHENS   Des. 85,010

CLOCK DIAL

Filed June 29, 1931

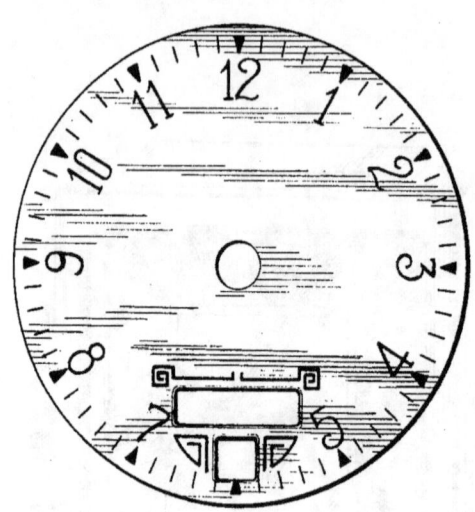

Inventor:
George H. Stephens
By Williams, Bradbury,
McCaleb & Hinkle.
Attys

Sept. 1, 1931.   G. H. STEPHENS   Des. 85,011
CLOCK CASE
Filed June 29, 1931

Inventor
George H. Stephens
By Williams, Bradbury,
McCaleb & Hinkle
Attys

Sept. 8, 1931.   R. D. BUDLONG   Des. 85,026
CLOCK CASE
Filed June 17, 1931

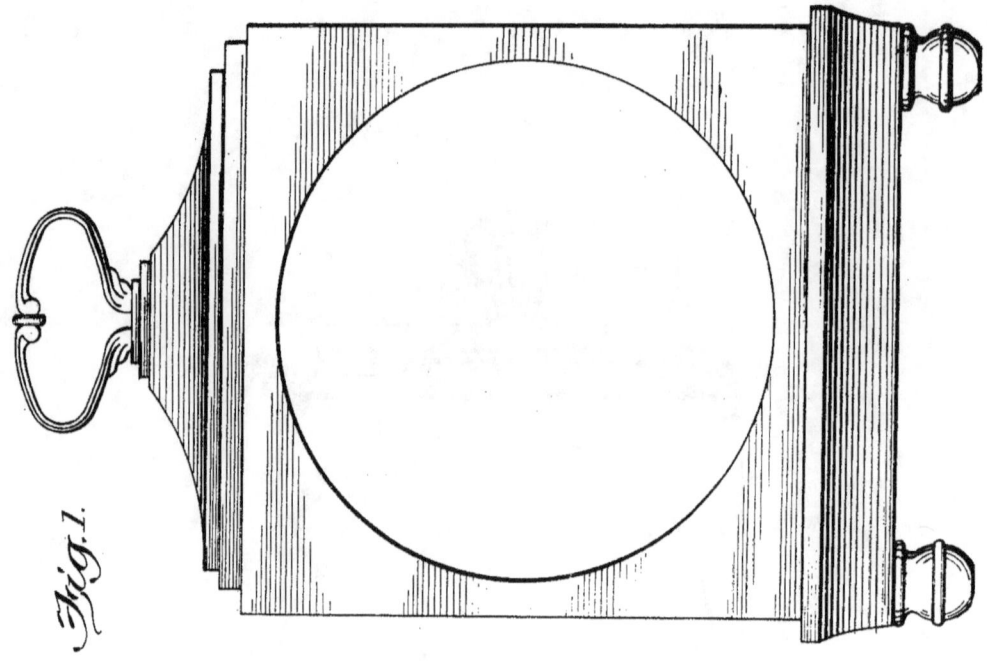

Fig. 1.

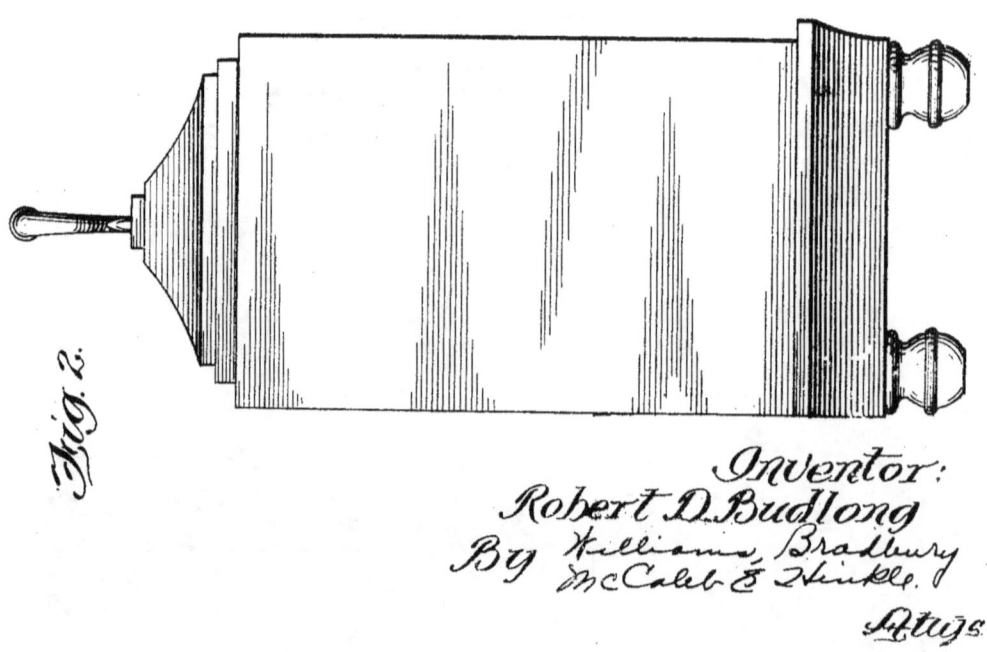

Fig. 2.

Inventor:
Robert D. Budlong
By Williams, Bradbury
McCaleb & Hinkle.
Attys

Sept. 8, 1931.   R. D. BUDLONG   Des. 85,027
CLOCK CASE
Filed June 29, 1931

Dec. 8, 1931. R. D. BUDLONG Des. 85,683
COMBINED DIAL AND HANDS FOR A CLOCK
Filed June 29, 1931

Inventor:
Robert D. Budlong
By Williams, Bradbury,
McCaleb & Hinkle,
Attys.

Dec 8, 1931.   G. H. STEPHENS ET AL   Des. 85,719
COMBINED DIAL AND HANDS FOR A CLOCK
Filed July 11, 1931

Inventors:
Robert D. Budlong
George H. Stephens
By Williams, Bradbury,
McCaleb & Hinkle
Attys.

March 15, 1932. G. H. STEPHENS Des. 86,546
CLOCK CASE
Filed June 29, 1931

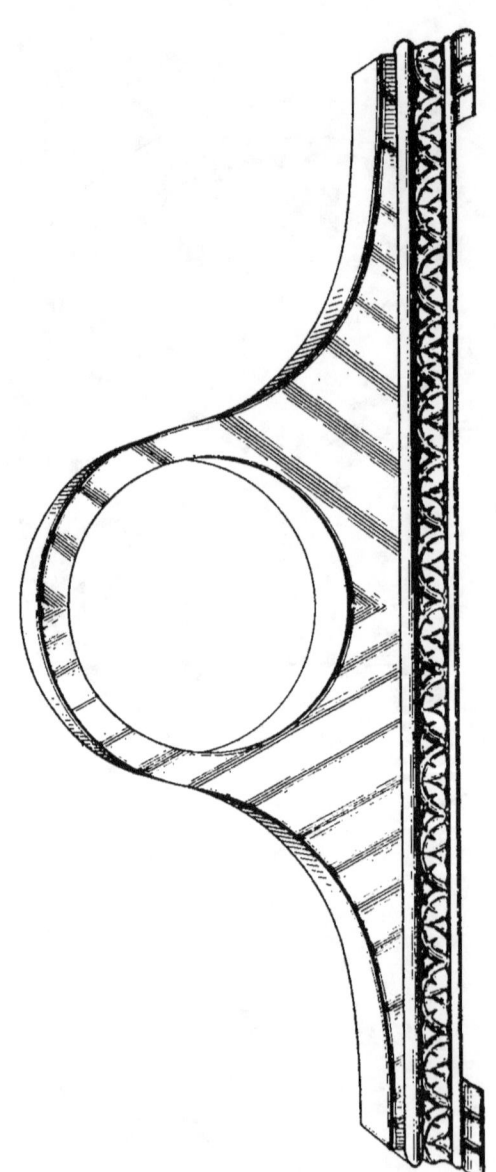

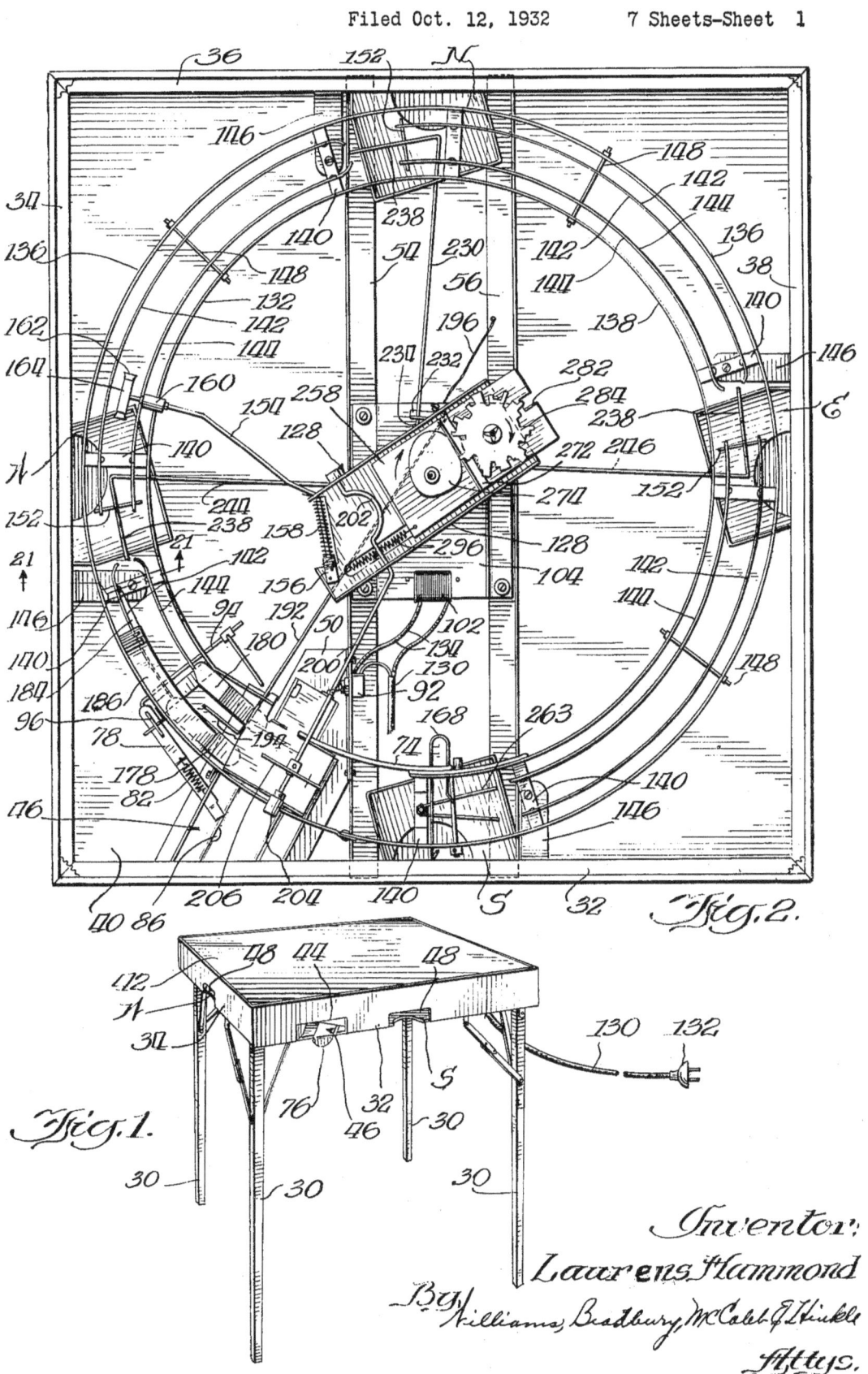

www.ingramcontent.com/pod-product-compliance
Lightning Source LLC
Chambersburg PA
CBHW081218230426
43666CB00015B/2793